FILMMAKERS SERIES
edited by
ANTHONY SLIDE

1. *James Whale*, by James Curtis. 1982
2. *Cinema Stylists*, by John Belton. 1983
3. *Harry Langdon*, by William Schelly. 1982
4. *William A. Wellman*, by Frank Thompson. 1983
5. *Stanley Donen*, by Joseph Casper. 1983
6. *Brian De Palma*, by Michael Bliss. 1983
7. *J. Stuart Blackton*, by Marian Blackton Trimble. 1985
8. *Martin Scorsese and Michael Cimino*, by Michael Bliss. 1985
9. *Franklin J. Schaffner*, by Erwin Kim. 1985
10. *D. W. Griffith and the Biograph Company*, by Cooper C. Graham et al. 1985
11. *Some Day We'll Laugh: An Autobiography*, by Esther Ralston. 1985
12. *The Memoirs of Alice Guy Blaché*, 2nd ed., translated by Roberta and Simone Blaché. 1996
13. *Leni Riefenstahl and Olympia*, by Cooper C. Graham. 1986
14. *Robert Florey*, by Brian Taves. 1987
15. *Henry King's America*, by Walter Coppedge. 1986
16. *Aldous Huxley and Film*, by Virginia M. Clark. 1987
17. *Five American Cinematographers*, by Scott Eyman. 1987
18. *Cinematographers on the Art and Craft of Cinematography*, by Anna Kate Sterling. 1987
19. *Stars of the Silents*, by Edward Wagenknecht. 1987
20. *Twentieth Century-Fox*, by Aubrey Solomon. 1988
21. *Highlights and Shadows: The Memoirs of a Hollywood Cameraman*, by Charles G. Clarke. 1989
22. *I Went That-a-Way: The Memoirs of a Western Film Director*, by Harry L. Fraser; edited by Wheeler Winston Dixon and Audrey Brown Fraser. 1990
23. *Order in the Universe: The Films of John Carpenter*, by Robert C. Cumbow. 1990 *(out of print; see No. 70)*
24. *The Films of Freddie Francis*, by Wheeler Winston Dixon. 1991
25. *Hollywood Be Thy Name*, by William Bakewell. 1991
26. *The Charm of Evil: The Life and Films of Terence Fisher*, by Wheeler Winston Dixon. 1991
27. *Lionheart in Hollywood: The Autobiography of Henry Wilcoxon*, with Katherine Orrison. 1991
28. *William Desmond Taylor: A Dossier*, by Bruce Long. 1991
29. *The Films of Leni Riefenstahl*, 2nd ed., by David B. Hinton. 1991
30. *Hollywood Holyland: The Filming and Scoring of "The Greatest Story Ever Told,"* by Ken Darby. 1992

31. *The Films of Reginald LeBorg: Interviews, Essays, and Filmography*, by Wheeler Winston Dixon. 1992
32. *Memoirs of a Professional Cad*, by George Sanders, with Tony Thomas. 1992
33. *The Holocaust in French Film*, by André Pierre Colombat. 1993
34. *Robert Goldstein and "The Spirit of '76,"* edited and compiled by Anthony Slide. 1993
35. *Those Were the Days, My Friend: My Life in Hollywood with David O. Selznick and Others*, by Paul Macnamara. 1993
36. *The Creative Producer*, by David Lewis, edited by James Curtis. 1993
37. *Reinventing Reality: The Art and Life of Rouben Mamoulian*, by Mark Spergel. 1993
38. *Malcolm St. Clair: His Films, 1915–1948*, by Ruth Anne Dwyer. 1997
39. *Beyond Hollywood's Grasp: American Filmmakers Abroad, 1914–1945*, by Harry Waldman. 1994
40. *A Steady Digression to a Fixed Point*, by Rose Hobart. 1994
41. *Radical Juxtaposition: The Films of Yvonne Rainer*, by Shelley Green. 1994
42. *Company of Heroes: My Life as an Actor in the John Ford Stock Company*, by Harry Carey Jr. 1994
43. *Strangers in Hollywood: A History of Scandinavian Actors in American Films from 1910 to World War II*, by Hans J. Wollstein. 1994
44. *Charlie Chaplin: Intimate Close-Ups*, by Georgia Hale, edited with an introduction and notes by Heather Kiernan. 1995
45. *The Word Made Flesh: Catholicism and Conflict in the Films of Martin Scorsese*, by Michael Bliss. 1995
46. *W. S. Van Dyke's Journal: White Shadows in the South Seas (1927–1928) and Other Van Dyke on Van Dyke*, edited and annotated by Rudy Behlmer. 1996
47. *Music from the House of Hammer: Music in the Hammer Horror Films, 1950–1980*, by Randall D. Larson. 1996
48. *Directing: Learn from the Masters*, by Tay Garnett. 1996
49. *Featured Player: An Oral Autobiography of Mae Clarke*, edited with an introduction by James Curtis. 1996
50. *A Great Lady: A Life of the Screenwriter Sonya Levien*, by Larry Ceplair. 1996
51. *A History of Horrors: The Rise and Fall of the House of Hammer*, by Denis Meikle. 1996
52. *The Films of Michael Powell and the Archers*, by Scott Salwolke. 1997

53. *From Oz to E.T.: Wally Worsley's Half-Century in Hollywood—A Memoir in Collaboration with Sue Dwiggins Worsley*, edited by Charles Ziarko. 1997

54. *Thorold Dickinson and the British Cinema*, by Jeffrey Richards. 1997

55. *The Films of Oliver Stone*, edited by Don Kunz. 1997

56. *Before, In, and After Hollywood: The Autobiography of Joseph E. Henabery*, edited by Anthony Slide. 1997

57. Ravished Armenia *and the Story of Aurora Mardiganian*, compiled by Anthony Slide. 1997

58. *Smile When the Raindrops Fall*, by Brian Anthony and Andy Edmonds. 1998

59. *Joseph H. Lewis: Overview, Interview, and Filmography*, by Francis M. Nevins. 1998

60. *September Song: An Intimate Biography of Walter Huston*, by John Weld. 1998

61. *Wife of the Life of the Party*, by Lita Grey Chaplin and Jeffrey Vance. 1998

62. *Down But Not Quite Out in Hollow-weird: A Documentary in Letters of Eric Knight*, by Geoff Gehman. 1998

63. *On Actors and Acting: Essays by Alexander Knox*, edited by Anthony Slide. 1998

64. *Back Lot: Growing Up with the Movies*, by Maurice Rapf. 1999

65. *Mr. Bernds Goes to Hollywood: My Early Life and Career in Sound Recording at Columbia with Frank Capra and Others*, by Edward Bernds. 1999

66. *Hugo Friedhofer: The Best Years of His Life: A Hollywood Master of Music for the Movies*, edited by Linda Danly. 1999

67. *Actors on Red Alert: Career Interviews with Five Actors and Actresses Affected by the Blacklist*, by Anthony Slide. 1999

68. *My Only Great Passion: The Life and Films of Carl Th. Dreyer*, by Jean Drum and Dale D. Drum. 1999

69. *Ready When You Are, Mr. Coppola, Mr. Spielberg, Mr. Crowe*, by Jerry Ziesmer. 1999

70. *Order in the Universe: The Films of John Carpenter*, 2nd ed., by Robert C. Cumbow. 2000

71. *Making Music with Charlie Chaplin*, by Eric James. 2000

72. *An Open Window: The Cinema of Victor Erice*, edited by Linda C. Ehrlich. 2000

73. *Satyajit Ray: In Search of the Modern*, by Suranjan Ganguly. 2000

74. *Voices from the Set: The* Film Heritage *Interviews*, edited by Tony Macklin and Nick Pici. 2000

75. *Paul Landres: A Director's Stories*, by Francis M. Nevins. 2000

76. *No Film in My Camera*, by Bill Gibson. 2000

77. *Saved from Oblivion: An Autobiography*, by Bernard Vorhaus. 2000
78. *Wolf Man's Maker: Memoir of a Hollywood Writer*, by Curt Siodmak. 2001
79. *An Actor, and a Rare One: Peter Cushing as Sherlock Holmes*, by Tony Earnshaw. 2001
80. *Picture Perfect*, by Herbert L. Strock. 2000
81. *Peter Greenaway's Postmodern/Poststructuralist Cinema*, edited by Paula Willoquet-Maricondi and Mary Alemany Galway. 2001
82. *Member of the Crew*, by Winfrid Kay Thackrey. 2001
83. *Barefoot on Barbed Wire*, by Jimmy Starr. 2001
84. *Henry Hathaway: A Directors Guild of America Oral History*, edited and annotated by Rudy Behlmer. 2001
85. *The Divine Comic: The Cinema of Roberto Benigni*, by Carlo Celli. 2001
86. *With or Without a Song: A Memoir*, by Edward Eliscu. 2001
87. *Stuart Erwin: The Invisible Actor*, by Judy Cornes. 2001
88. *Some Cutting Remarks: Seventy Years a Film Editor*, by Ralph E. Winters. 2001
89. *Confessions of a Hollywood Director*, by Richard L. Bare. 2001
90. *Peckinpah's Women: A Reappraisal of the Portrayal of Women in the Period Westerns of Sam Peckinpah*, by Bill Mesce Jr. 2001
91. *Budd Schulberg: A Bio-Bibliography*, by Nicholas Beck. 2001
92. *Between the Bullets: The Spiritual Cinema of John Woo*, by Michael Bliss. 2002
93. *The Hollywood I Knew: 1916–1988*, by Herbert Coleman. 2002
94. *The Films of Steven Spielberg*, edited by Charles L. P. Silet. 2002
95. *Hitchcock and the Making of Marnie*, by Tony Lee Moral. 2002
96. *White Horse, Black Hat: A Quarter Century on Hollywood's Poverty Row*, by C. Jack Lewis. 2002
97. *Worms in the Winecup: A Memoir*, by John Bright. 2002
98. *Straight from the Horse's Mouth: Ronald Neame, An Autobiography*, by Ronald Neame. 2003
99. *Reach for the Top: The Turbulent Life of Laurence Harvey*, by Anne Sinai. 2003
100. *Jackie Coogan: The World's Boy King: A Biography of Hollywood's Legendary Child Star*, by Diana Serra Cary. 2003
101. *Rungs on a Ladder: Hammer Films Seen through a Soft Gauze*, by Christopher Neame. 2003
102. *The Classically American Comedy of Larry Gelbart*, by Jay Malarcher. 2003
103. *Perpetually Cool: The Many Lives of Anna May Wong (1905–1961)*, by Anthony B. Chan. 2003
104. *Irene Dunne: The First Lady of Hollywood*, by Wes D. Gehring. 2003

105. *Scorsese Up Close: A Study of the Films*, by Ben Nyce. 2004
106. *Hitchcock and Poe: The Legacy of Delight and Terror*, by Dennis R. Perry. 2003
107. *Life Is Beautiful, but Not for Jews: Another View of the Film by Benigni*, by Kobi Niv, translated by Jonathan Beyrak Lev. 2003
108. *Young Man in Movieland*, by Jan Read. 2004
109. *A Cast of Shadows*, by Ronnie Maasz. 2004

Scorsese Up Close

A Study of the Films

Ben Nyce

Filmmakers Series, No. 105

The Scarecrow Press, Inc.
Lanham, Maryland, and Oxford
2004

SCARECROW PRESS, INC.

Published in the United States of America
by Scarecrow Press, Inc.
A wholly owned subsidiary of
The Rowman & Littlefield Publishing Group, Inc.
4501 Forbes Boulevard, Suite 200, Lanham, Maryland 20706
www.scarecrowpress.com

PO Box 317
Oxford
OX2 9RU, UK

British Library Cataloguing in Publication Information Available

Library of Congress Cataloging-in-Publication Data

Nyce, Ben.
  Scorsese up close : a study of the films / Ben Nyce.
    p. cm. — (Filmmakers series ; no. 105)
  Includes bibliographical references and index.
  ISBN 0-8108-4787-6 (alk. paper)
  1. Scorsese, Martin–Criticism and interpretation. I. Title.
II. Series.
PN1998.3.S39 N93 2004
791.4302'33'092–dc22   2003020840

Once more for Ann, Kate, and Chris

Contents

Acknowledgments   xiii
To the Reader   xv

Chapter 1: Beginnings   1
    WHAT'S A NICE GIRL LIKE YOU DOING IN A PLACE
    LIKE THIS?; IT'S NOT JUST YOU, MURRAY!; THE BIG
    SHAVE; WHO'S THAT KNOCKING AT MY DOOR?;
    BOX CAR BERTHA

Chapter 2: A New Voice   21
    MEAN STREETS; ITALIANAMERICAN

Chapter 3: A Career Choice   31
    ALICE DOESN'T LIVE HERE ANYMORE

Chapter 4: The Strange and Familiar   37
    TAXI DRIVER

Chapter 5: A New, New Musical   51
    NEW YORK, NEW YORK; THE LAST WALTZ;
    AMERICAN BOY

Chapter 6: Bloodrope   65
    RAGING BULL

Chapter 7: Empty Spaces   77
    THE KING OF COMEDY

Chapter 8: Bad Ladies   85
      AFTER HOURS

Chapter 9: An Homage and a Career Choice   93
      THE COLOR OF MONEY

Chapter 10: The Agony on the Hill   101
      THE LAST TEMPTATION OF CHRIST

Chapter 11: The Artist as Agonist   109
      LIFE LESSONS

Chapter 12: The Real Crew   115
      GOODFELLAS

Chapter 13: Prelude to Rape   125
      CAPE FEAR

Chapter 14: A Life Unlived   131
      THE AGE OF INNOCENCE

Chapter 15: The Mob Again   139
      CASINO

Chapter 16: The Buddhist Soul   147
      KUNDUN

Chapter 17: The Urban Saint   155
      BRINGING OUT THE DEAD

Conclusion   163
Postscript: *GANGS OF NEW YORK*   165
Bibliography   169
Index   173

Acknowledgments

Scorsese Up Close began in my film courses at the University of San Diego. For three years my students and I selected four or five Scorsese films to scrutinize each semester, and their questions and perceptions added a lot to my understanding of the films. My gratitude goes first of all to them. Support from USD in the form of faculty research grants helped to complete the project. Monica Wagner, Vivian Holland, and Ann Pantano assisted greatly in manuscript preparation. Tony Slide, the filmmaker series editor at Scarecrow, gave the manuscript a close critical reading with useful suggestions, and Rebecca Massa helped with publication. My wife, Ann Gardner, gave criticism and immeasurable support.

To the Reader

This brief study of Martin Scorsese's films is intended as a close look at his cinematic text. Many film studies discuss their subject at arm's length. The story is summarized, the underlying themes discussed, perhaps a crucial moment in the plot is analyzed. Particular shots and sequences of shots are often left unexamined. No good studies of works of literature operate on such a general level. There's a reason for this, of course: film flows by so quickly and works on the viewer so subliminally that many details are not consciously noticed or examined. Even though we have VCRs and DVDs which allow us to go back and look at an intriguing moment, we prefer, on the whole, to "go with the flow." It's a lot easier to flip back a few pages to a particular passage in a book.

My purpose is to bring to Scorsese's films something close to the same scrutiny which he brings to the shooting and editing of a film. I try to treat the film as a whole (as a story which flows by, captivating the general viewer) and also discuss specific shots and sequences in which Scorsese can be seen enacting his craft at the highest level (the sequences that film buffs and film students like to go back to because they are equally captivating). I think of my audience as containing both average filmgoers and students of film. In fact, the average filmgoer in the '90s is much more sophisticated than those filmgoers who said they couldn't understand Welles' *The Magnificent Ambersons* when they filled out their preview cards at the Fox theater in Pomona in 1942—which resulted in the wholesale dismemberment of the film while Welles was away. Hopefully, this book can speak to them, too. The basic strategy is to examine how, in the visuals and soundtrack, Scorsese dramatizes his vision. An attempt is made to examine in detail at least one or two key sequences in each film.

As Scorsese matures as a film director he has increasingly demonstrated a range of sensibility and technique that one would not have expected. His later films, *The Age of Innocence* and *Kundun*, bear his mark, but they're also by a different director—a man willing to take risks and stretch himself in his choice of subject. Scorsese has always brought a religious dedication to film but his earlier work (*Mean Streets, Taxi Driver, Raging Bull, Goodfellas*) seemed permanently based in contemporary urban violence. After the dead ends of *Casino* and *Cape Fear* it looked as if he might not have much more to say. True artist that he is, he then moved into fresh areas—in *Kundun* in particular, with its evocation of Buddhist spiritual growth. He's on a personal and artistic quest. This study stays close to the films themselves; it doesn't discuss the often lengthy process of arranging for a film to be made, and it doesn't discuss abandoned projects or biographical details. These important subjects are treated by Friedman, Keyser, Kelly, and others—as well as by Scorsese himself.

I'm interested in Scorsese's artistic quest. This study discusses his films chronologically, a section to each major film. In the conclusion I try to sum up Scorsese's achievement.

Chapter 1

BEGINNINGS

WHAT'S A NICE GIRL LIKE YOU DOING IN
A PLACE LIKE THIS? 1963;
IT'S NOT JUST YOU, MURRAY! 1964;
THE BIG SHAVE, 1967; WHO'S THAT
KNOCKING AT MY DOOR? 1969;
BOXCAR BERTHA, 1972

Martin Scorsese was born in 1942 in Flushing, Long Island, to a working-class family. His parents, Charles and Catherine Scorsese, were children of Sicilian immigrants. Like his father, who sold men's clothes, Charles worked in the clothing trade as a presser. Catherine did sewing at home, having learned the skill from her mother. The family suffered economic reversal at one point and had to move away from Elizabeth Street in "Little Italy," where Charles and Catherine had been born, before they were able to return. In *Scorsese on Scorsese*, the best source of information on his early life along with the film *Italianamerican*, Scorsese describes the environment:

1

At this time the Italian-American community lived in a series of about
ten blocks, starting from Houston Street down to Chinatown at Canal
Street. The three main blocks were on Elizabeth Street, Mott Street and
Mulberry Street. Little Italy was very sharply defined, so often the
people from one block wouldn't hang out with those from another.
Elizabeth Street was mainly Sicilian, as were my grandparents, and here
the people had their own regulations and laws. We didn't care about the
Government, or politicians or the police: we felt we were right in our
ways.[1]

The enclosed nature of this life is indicated by Scorsese's remark that
when he first went to New York University, only a few blocks away in
Greenwich Village, he had only been in the area once before.[2] Like Charlie
in *Mean Streets* his imagination was limited to a particular life in a
confined area. The main role models in the area were priests and mobsters:
"In my neighborhood, the people in power were the tough guys on the
street, and the Church. The organized crime figures would tip their hats to
a priest and watch their language, and they would have their cars and pets
blessed. This may have had something to do with my decision, when I was
eight or nine, that I wanted to become a priest. At any rate it lasted right
up until the time I made my first movie."[3] A somewhat frail boy with severe asthma, he wore a leather jacket and fantasized, as all boys do, about
being a tough guy (hence the preoccupation with the mob in many of his
films) but was drawn to the priesthood for its spiritual and intellectual life
as well as the deference (more likely lip service) paid by the toughs. This
environment counts in many ways for the mixture of the spiritual and the
violent in his films. It also counts for the almost religious dedication he
brings to film making. Like James Joyce, his art became his religion.
        Even in hard times his father and sometimes his mother had money for
the movies. He saw Michael Powell and Emeric Pressburger's *The Thief
of Baghdad* at age six, an overwhelming experience, and later their *The
Red Shoes*. He would watch some films over and over again on television
to his parents' irritation. This immersion in moving images grew directly
out of his childhood interest in painting and drawing, making up his own
stories and rendering them in comic book-like sequences—an early
version of the storyboard. But he was a distracted student and only went
to NYU because he couldn't get into Jesuit University at Fordham and
because NYU had film classes. He was still thinking of returning to his
seminary studies when he took Haig Manoogian's film class and became
inspired to not only study films but make them. Manoogian chose him
from among his many students to create his first short films at NYU and

later he produced his first feature film, *Who's That Knocking at My Door?* (1969). Scorsese dedicated *Raging Bull* to him. As a film student in the early '60s he was influenced by the French New Wave work ofChabrol, Resnais, Rohmer, Truffaut, Godard—as well as the Italian cinema of DeSica, Rossellini, Antonioni, and Fellini. He however resisted the idea that American film was inferior when he briefly became an instructor at NYU, championing the work of Hawks, Ford, Minnelli, and Welles, among many others. As a result of his early academic endeavors, Scorsese has always been a student of film, drawing attention to neglected filmmakers, championing film preservation, fighting colorization, and generally acting as a kind of dean of American film culture. He's the first of our major directors to take on such wide-ranging responsibilities.

What's a Nice Girl Like You Doing in a Place Like This?

The first of his short student films made at NYU in 1963 is the nine-minute *What's a Nice Girl Like You Doing in a Place Like This?* It's a comic treatment of obsession with lots of clever, though not particularly original, visuals. The central character, Harry, is a writer who comes to the city, buys a picture to decorate his apartment, and becomes so obsessed with it that he disappears into the picture. It's a statement about the isolation of the writer and the power of the visual. There are some interesting sequences, particularly in the first full presentation of the picture which consists of six shots. In the first we see a man who looks very much like Harry standing in a boat on a lake near the shore. In the second he and the boat are gone and the third shows Harry but no boat. The fourth and fifth repeat the first and second, and the sixth pulls back to give us the framed picture of Harry, the boat, and the lake. What is the picture really like? We can't be sure. It's a subjective sequence in which Harry alternates between reading himself into the picture and removing himself. It's also a nice statement on the indeterminate nature of reality. Harry needs the picture for inspiration, but it also traps him, causing writer's block. He spends his time watching TV and there's a fine shot as he sits in the darkened room in the glow from the screen, his eyes slowly pivoting away as the rising camera follows their motion toward the picture. He's only rescued by a woman who inserts herself between him and the picture. He marries her but his obsession returns and his analyst gives him the unhelpful advice to deal with his obsession with the picture by "staring

it down." A friend who comes looking for him finds him waving franti-
cally from within the lake.

   This little film has the feeling of careful planning. No single shot
lacks function and many are playful and witty as befits a young artist
playing around with the form. When Harry says he's just hanging around
his apartment we see a corny shot of him hanging from the suit rack in his
closet, and when he tells us he and his wife visited the world's fair on their
honeymoon we see shots of them at the construction site for the fair. It's
a light-hearted treatment of self-destructive behavior which Scorsese
would examine in his later work.

It's Not Just You, Murray!

At fifteen minutes, *It's Not Just You, Murray!* (1964) is the longest and
least effective of Scorsese's student films. It's a portrait of Murray, a
small-time promoter who likes to pretend he's been a successful theatrical
producer, but who is so obsessed with the idea of his friend Joe's loyalty
that he willfully disregards Joe's manipulations and betrayals. The script
by Scorsese and Mardik Martin has a loose, grab-bag quality. The film
opens strongly with Murray ingratiatingly presenting to us the material
tokens of the sweet life he has achieved only because of Joe. He asks Joe
for validation of this idea and Joe, casually playing pool in another
location, barks out "Yeah." But Murray isn't fully persuaded he's making
a convincing impression on us and instructs the cameraman to stop and
start over. His insecurity and need for delusional behavior are presented
in a few shots.

   The rest of the film deviates from this economy. We're given a
lengthy sequence of Murray and Joe as bootleggers, with Murray doing all
the dirty work while Joe shouts instructions, and a Keystone Kops like raid
after which Murray goes to jail while Joe remains free. The mob muscles
in and Murray is beaten up and has his feet put in cement while Joe tells
him to stay cool. This sequence is a comic parody of mob films and
Scorsese's first treatment of gangland behavior. After Murray marries the
nurse he meets during his stay in the hospital, Joe begins an affair with her
and the two men embark upon a series of theatrical productions beginning
with "Life Is a Gazelle," from which we see one full singing and dancing
number (with students and costumes from NYU's theater department, one
imagines) with a Busby Berkeley-like kaleidoscope passage of the
dancers—another parody. Murray's addiction to platitudinous philoso-

phizing, in this instance about how life has changed for the better, gives us a series of not-so-very-funny visuals: change in motels is depicted by a line of whores standing outside a motel; the rise of Japanese imports by a shot of Abraham Lincoln in the Lincoln Memorial with "made in Japan" inscribed on the marble arm rest. Murray then appears as a defendant before the House Unamerican Activities Committee with Joe at his elbow. There are a series of still shots of Joe as a young man looking decidedly diabolic while Murray continues to praise him. A reason for Murray's obtuseness occurs in the several appearances of his mother, played by Scorsese's mom, Catherine, who constantly offers him food, feeding him through the wire mesh of his jail cell on one occasion. He hasn't grown up. Finally there's a confrontation in which Murray accuses Joe of betrayal without looking at him. We don't know what has brought this on but listen to Joe's endless explanations until Scorsese's voice suddenly breaks in saying "cut the sound" and Joe goes on in silence. The breaking of what narrative fabric there is at this point is a surprise and a relief. We're tired of Joe's deceptions but even more tired of Murray's blindness. Scorsese's intervention reminds us that he's an active though unseen player. Probably the most technically impressive aspect of the film is its varied sound mix, including the coordination of a strong music score, rapid dialogue and voice-over, and ambient as well as artificial sound. The end of the film skirts any consideration of Murray's possible awakening. Scorsese has said, "I just couldn't figure out how to end it."[4] With a lengthy quote from the ending of Fellini's *8 1/2*, Murray and Joe, standing in Murray's Cadillac convertible, direct the whole company in a celebratory procession of communal enjoyment. Perhaps it's a fitting closure to a short film which feels long and overly inclusive. Murray is wearing the same black hat with broad rolled-up brim that Mastroianni wears as Fellini's alter ego.

The Big Shave

No short film contains the essence of what's to come like *The Big Shave*, made in 1967, and by far Scorsese's best early effort. It's also the shortest at six minutes. It employs the simplest of means to attain its power. We see a young man enter a white bathroom, prepare to shave, and then proceed to scrape his face and neck with a safety razor so badly that he ends up a bloody mess. This action is performed in a single setting in real time to the continuous, unedited sound of Bunny Berrigan's classic "I Can't Get

Started." The effect is bizarre, disturbing, and perhaps "humorously macabre."[5] The obsessive, self-destructive behavior we've noticed in the earlier shorts, and which becomes a major concern in later films, is given full, all-consuming depiction. What appears at first to be a documentary (almost like an instruction manual on how to shave) turns into an expressionist nightmare. The mundane real, which Scorsese had emphasized mainly in the documentary street shots of Little Italy in the earlier shorts, gradually transforms into expressionist fantasy. *The Big Shave* points forward to *Taxi Driver*, *Raging Bull*, and *Life Lessons*, among others, in its combination of documentary realism and expressionism.

One of the most powerful elements in the film is its use of color. The bathroom is nearly all white, except for the gleaming silver of the chrome fixtures and the mirror which at one point begins to dissolve into whiteness. The title of the film emerges from a white background and then disappears into it. As the man begins to bleed more heavily, the red blood seems at first to violate this purity or this nothingness and then to subsume it. We first see a low shot of the white floor, toilet, and shower curtain. There's nice cutting on the chrome sink fixtures to the rhythm of Berrigan's obligato on the horn before he begins his vocal solo. The man enters, washes his face, and then removes his white T-shirt. Scorsese gives us three rhythmic shots from different angles which repeat the gesture of removing the shirt—a nice tribute to Godard. The camera closes in as shaving cream is applied and the razoring begins. Extreme close-ups show the man touching his face with his hand to see if the shave has been successful. He moves his head relaxedly as he checks; there's no expression in his face. Indeed his face is blank throughout the film. He doesn't act at all; his actions do the work. He lathers again and begins to shave, this time with more pressure, and the cutting speeds up. We begin to notice small blood marks, then streaks of blood. There's no expression of pain in the man's face as he persists. We notice small drops of blood as the camera looks down at the white sink then larger gouts. Finally, when his face and neck are streaming red, he makes the suicidal gesture of sweeping the razor across his neck. This movement is done in three shot again though here the gesture is divided into three segments, not repeated. The white sink is now nearly obliterated in red. There's a low shot of his bare feet with blood on them as the music stops. The final three shots show him doing touch-up with the razor, rivulets of blood running down his chest, and then laying the razor carefully in the sink. He's clearly going to survive.

The effect of Berrigan's music is bizarre. The lyrics speak of being unable to woo the beloved successfully but they're voiced, like many blues, in an upbeat and sprightly manner, particularly in Berrigan's horn solos. Here the "can't get started" translates to can't stop. The strange coupling of the dogged, depressed actions of the shaver and the music undoubtedly provides what humor there is. In its increasingly dream-like images, it's a film designed to enter the subconscious.

As a final note the credits cite Herman Melville on whiteness and "Viet 67." The Melville reference shows Scorsese's literary dimension and the "Viet 67" indicates that he thought of the film as a protest against the war in Vietnam. Certainly the country was involved in a self-destructive and bloody enterprise.

Who's That Knocking at My Door?

Who's That Knocking at My Door? (1969), Scorsese's first feature-length film, did not establish him as a filmmaker to be reckoned with, but it's as important as *Mean Streets* in his development, though it's often given scant attention. The film went through a series of versions (first as *Bring on the Dancing Girls* in 1965, then as *I Call First* in 1967). Funded in part by Scorsese's film instructor at NYU, Haig Manoogian, and his wife, Betzi, the film remained undistributed until Scorsese agreed to add an explicit sex sequence. According to Les Keyser, Scorsese and his lead actor, Harvey Keitel, flew to Amsterdam where they shot extended nude scenes between Keitel and an actress who had appeared in one of Godard's films. With this footage incorporated, distributor Joseph Brennen finally released the film.[6]

Who's That Knocking is a probing examination of one man's conflicted sexuality. It also establishes several issues Scorsese will pursue through the rest of his career, most notably the connection between religion and violence, and the difficulty of leading a moral life without withdrawing from a corrupt world. Cinematically, the film uses strategies Scorsese employs for the first time and which become elements of his signature, most notably improvisation between actors and the use of popular music. Most of all, it's a film about the excitements and confusions of youth. Its execution is sometimes crude, even amateurish, but it contains passages of surprising power and sophistication, revealing the filmmaker Scorsese was to become. Like almost all of his work, it's fresh and direct—from the gut.

The film involves the attraction the central character J.R. (Harvey Keitel, who will repeat the role in *Mean Streets*) experiences toward a sweet blonde woman known only as "the girl," played by Zina Bethune. We see them meet, fall in love, and break apart. The major part of the film involves sequences in which J.R. relives experiences with the girl while he is hanging out with his buddies in bars, cars, or in the 8th Ward Pleasure Club. His pals are irritated that they don't have his full attention. They exist in a state of protracted adolescence which J.R. has a chance to break free from. His failure to do so is caused partially by his inability to overcome the girl's confession to him that she's not a virgin because she had been raped. In his rigid Catholic upbringing women are either girls or whores. He can't accept someone who has been dirtied even though he loves her.

Two sequences at the very start of the film, before the credits, pose the problem concisely. In the first, the camera pans around a kitchen as a mother (Catherine Scorsese, in the second of many short roles in her son's films) makes dinner. The first image we see is a statue of the Virgin Mary with halo as she holds a child. The camera then moves to Momma cooking dinner. Later in the sequence there is a dissolve from the statue to Momma serving food to small children. The only odd element here is the sound-track which has the steady rhythmic beat of machinery—as if some kind of overdetermined behavior is being created. Is this a shot of J.R.'s childhood? We can't be sure, but it's a reasonable guess.

The next sequence involves street violence among young men. We see J.R. leaning forward smiling as he looks at a frightened youngster who may be Puerto Rican or at least Latino and who wears a headband. J.R.'s friend Joey conceals a metal bar behind his back. The Latino kisses the cross around his neck before the attack begins and he's knocked down and kicked along the sidewalk to the delight of his attackers, J.R. and his pals, accompanied by an upbeat rock song.

The connection between these two sequences isn't hard to grasp. The childhood kitchen is both comforting and claustrophobic. A young man grows up and away from it by proving himself in the streets. The testing ground is extreme (deadly violence) because the pull of the mother (the mother who cooks and serves and the mother of Christ) is so powerful. The street violence has a religious dimension (the kissing of the cross) for the Latino victim who calls on God to protect him in the unequal fight but also for J.R. who, though he doesn't know it, is testing the limits of his devotion to God's law by his decidedly unchristian behavior. Is he going to be a good boy, a model Christian—possibly even a priest—or a thug, a tough guy? As I've pointed out, these were the questions disturbing Scorsese's youth. J.R. is trying to find out who he is throughout the film. In this sense the film's title has something to do with the strange other unknown figure who knocks on the door. The title poses the question "Who is the real me?"

As a mothered boy J.R. is particularly drawn to macho role models. That's why he keeps bringing up John Wayne in *The Searchers* when he first meets the girl. A thoughtful and intellectually curious person, she's been reading *Paris Match* and J.R. notices Wayne's photo. He immediately attempts to establish himself as an authority by telling her twice that *cicatrice* is Spanish for scar and that Western movies "would solve everybody's problems" (particularly, one might add, his own). Rather than be put off, she's charmed by his aggressive and entertaining energy. He's a movie buff, full of enthusiasm about all aspects of film. The Wayne references spring up later in a decidedly less friendly context when we see J.R. and his buddies at the Pleasure Club. Dressed in coats and ties they're all half drunk, shoving each other around, full of careless laughter. One of the bigger, meaner guys pulls out a very small handgun (a larger gun has earlier been passed around) and begins to rough up Sally Ga Ga, a friend of J.R.'s who always seems to be pushed around. General laughter accompanies this scene, even as Sally appears more and more terrorized.

Finally the mean guy takes aim at some liquor bottles and blasts them (a standard trope from Westerns) and we realize he hasn't been brandishing a toy gun. At this point Scorsese interjects still shots of Wayne from *Rio Bravo*, along with shots of Dean Martin, Angie Dickinson, and Ricky Nelson from the film. The import of the Wayne shots is different than their earlier use, when they are associated with J.R.'s enthusiasm for Westerns. Here they seem to validate the brutality and danger of the bully. The early shots are from within J.R., the later ones are from Scorsese. They're like the upbeat musical accompaniment to the street violence we've seen earlier. J.R.'s need for macho role models is shared by Scorsese. He's aware of this need but unable to distance himself from it. In this sense *Who's That Knocking* is about youth by youth. The *Rio Bravo* shots conclude with a nice transition to a poster of the film outside a theater where J.R. has just taken (dragged?) the girl to see it. J.R. is doing all the talking.

The sex sequence that follows is particularly interesting in its indication of the influence of French new wave directors, particularly Godard. The use of triple shots (the woman's naked leg is shown making the same movement three times) and certain camera movements are almost direct quotes. Later shots such as J.R.'s bleeding mouth after he kisses the crucifix are right out of Bergman. They show that, as Scorsese has remarked, his cinematic eye was looking both east and west—toward Truffaut and Godard as well as Ford and Hawks. J.R. is Scorsese's Antoine Doinel, Truffaut's autobiographical hero in several films.

A more seasoned director might have omitted the long episode in which J.R. and his closest pal, Joey, take a trip to Copake, New York, where they climb a mountain and watch the sunset. The import seems to be that J.R. is open to nature's grandeur while Joey is locked tight in his city mentality. This is the only extended sequence in a Scorsese film in which the natural environment is explored for its own sake and for its spiritual dimension (the natural setting of *Cape Fear* is handled purely for purposes of creating excitement). Given the personal character of *Who's That Knocking*, it's interesting that Scorsese doesn't pursue the subject of nature in the rest of his work. He's a city boy to the end, with a fast moving eye, an agitated rhythm. This is both a strength and a limitation, particularly given an American cinema (and literature) full of the enigmatic poetry of natural landscape.

The girl's confession to J.R. about her rape is a huge mistake on her part. She already knows about his idea of nice girls and whores. It's as if, in her love for J.R., she overlooks it or expects that he can get beyond it for her. The confession is preceded by J.R.'s criticism of her for placing a holy candle on the dinner table (in the opening sequence of Momma in the kitchen there's a shot of the candle). It's a note of warning of what's to come. The confession is intercut by brief sequences of the violent rape. These images have a realistic quality and evidently come from within the girl as she tells her story. They suggest that she hasn't been badly damaged by the experience. It's she who wants to have sex with J.R., while he constantly pulls away in their earlier foreplay. Later images of the rape from within J.R. have a more lurid, expressionist quality. Though not the one raped, he can't handle it while she can. J.R.'s reaction to the confession is full of disbelief: "how can I believe you," "how do I know you didn't go through the same story with him" (the rapist). He's more concerned with his own hurt than with hers. There's a frantic quality to his celebratory behavior in a bar with his pals after he leaves the girl.

By today's standards the girl seems unevolved. She doesn't seem much particularized beyond her generic name. She's not even Cindy or Mary Lou. She doesn't take a cheerfully mordant view of the machismo and all it conceals. She doesn't appear to have any strong ideas of her own, despite the fact that she's intelligent and thoughtful. She doesn't even kid around and poke fun at J.R. in a kindly way. She's evidently looking for a man to complete her life. Only at the end, when J.R. tells her he forgives her and will marry her, does she show toughness and assertiveness as she tells him to leave. The film isn't really interested in her as a developing character, though it would have had a more complex dimension had it shown how a strong woman's agency helps a young man grow up. Scorsese wants to keep the focus on J.R. and his problems before he grows into the more mature J.R. of *Mean Streets*.

If the girl isn't a helper she *is* a threat, in spite of her unassertiveness, first because she asks J.R. to grow up (particularly by her confession) and because she asks him to leave the safety of his pals. The male bonding we see in *Who's That Knocking* isn't the more mature variety we see in a film such as *Smoke*; it's adolescent bonding in which the members of the group are particularly sensitive to any attempt by a woman to pull one of them away. The threat is also sexual. J.R. can "perform" with a whore but has trouble with a good girl. Before he learns that the girl isn't a virgin he acts like he's one. The girl confronts him with his deeply divided sexuality. He's also threatened intellectually which he shows when he calls her a "brain" in the final breakup scene. He fears a strong woman. Her more wide-ranging interests (extending well beyond Westerns) and her greater maturity are both attractive to him—as well as unsettling in the crunch.

She confronts him with the anxiety of growth. As a personal statement, the film suggests that Scorsese himself was threatened by a strong woman. There's both weakness *and* courage in this statement.

J.R. is much more comfortable playing the role of conciliator when his pals bring back two young women and each begins to be seduced by one of the group in separate bedrooms. The others joke around in an outer room playing a game of "I call first" (the early title) to see who gets to have sex with a girl first, after she's sufficiently aroused. When the gang crashes into the bedrooms and begins to rough up the women, J.R. intervenes and prevents them from being injured as they leave crying. This is the mediating role we see him perform throughout *Mean Streets*. He's much stronger with his pals than with a maturing woman.

Cinematically, *Who's That Knocking* is somewhat cumbersome, as I've suggested. Still a short sequence midway through the film has the kind of power demonstrated in later efforts. Joey leads J.R. back to his apartment after he's gotten very drunk in the aftermath of the confession. In seven brief shots Scorsese shows the tortured love J.R. feels for the girl. After Joey opens the door to the apartment hallway and then leaves in shot 1, J.R. walks in the door and stands dazed against the wall in 2. There's a cut to a close-up of J.R.'s face in 3 which accentuates his semi-conscious state. He slides down the wall in a medium shot in 4 and the slide is continued until he's sitting on the floor in a nicely timed overhead shot in 5. In 6 he reaches out his hand and this shot is spliced into the same hand movement as he reaches to touch the girl's hair in 7. It's a quiet, potent passage without the accompaniment of popular music and it evokes J.R.'s constant preoccupation with the girl far better than many other sequences with her which seem crudely forced into the goings on between him and the guys.

The absence of popular music in this sequence underlines its use throughout much of the film—a pattern which will become a Scorsese trademark in some of his finest work such as *Raging Bull* and *Goodfellas*. The use of popular song serves to place the audience in a specific era as well as to give emotional accent to the action. Sometimes it appears as if particular shots and sequences take their rhythm from the music rather than the other way around. Certain films like *Taxi Driver* and *The Age of Innocence* have entire scores prepared for them while others like *Raging Bull* and *Goodfellas* rely on popular song. Some viewers find an overuse of such song while others feel it's entirely appropriate. In Scorsese's usually fast-paced sequences, popular song seems highly effective as an accompaniment and even as commentary on the action. The source of its use can be seen in the following comment:

> I was living in a very crowded area where music would be playing constantly from various apartments across the street, from bars and candy stores. The radio was always on; a juke box would be playing out over the street; and in the tenement areas you'd hear opera from one room, Benny Goodman from another, and rock and roll from downstairs.[7]

This environment undoubtedly accounts for Scorsese's preference for a pastiche of musical quotes rather than for what is known in the trade as "through music"—a score by a single composer which accompanies the images. Only a few of his films—*Taxi Driver, The Last Temptation of Christ, Cape Fear, The Age of Innocence,* and *Kundun*—have through music, and *Taxi Driver* and *Cape Fear* use it because Scorsese wanted a score by film's greatest composer Bernard Herrmann. A good essay on Scorsese's use of music would be worth doing.

The other signature element we first encounter in *Who's That Knocking* is the use of improvisation between actors. The freshness and honesty of the film are achieved here. Many of the group scenes with J.R. and his pals seem highly improvised, particularly the scene which culminates in the bottle shooting, and the sequence in which J.R. gets drunk at a bar with Joey and Sally Ga Ga after the confession. There's almost no dialogue in these sequences, however. A better example is the long breakup scene with the girl. The key lines of the scene must have been established ("It's going to be alright now; I understand and I forgive you") but within a basic structure Scorsese gives Keitel and Bethune plenty of room for spontaneous statement and response. The purpose is, of course, to avoid the potentially airless effect of actors repeating memorized lines to each other. From the standpoint of strict verbal economy the scene goes on a bit too long but it has the feeling of real life. We see J.R. both attacking and attempting to mollify the girl ("I'm sorry I didn't mean it. I'm so confused by this whole thing") while she moves from tenderness and passivity ("well, it's sort of your decision whether you love me enough") to suspicion to outright rejection. The light, quick movement of the cameras assisted by the editing exactly capture the fluid, confused, and shattering ending to the relationship. The use of improvisation will get Scorsese into trouble in *New York, New York* but it immeasurably enhances the films that follow *Who's That Knocking.*

The ending of the film is an avalanche of cinematic images, sixty shots in which we see J.R.'s torment in full flood. He's in the confessional attempting to purge his guilt, and perhaps to discover how he has arrived where he is. The sixty shots which occur quickly are an attempt to get inside J.R.'s head and depict his raging consciousness. His words of contrition are voiced mechanically but the images suggest deep disturbance. We have shots in increasing close-up of his kissing the girl then shots of a statue of the Virgin Mary in the church, shots from the sex sequence, the Virgin Mary again, the girl's rape, the Virgin, a close-up of the wounds of Christ as he lies deposed across Mary's lap, J.R.'s bleeding mouth as he kisses the crucifix, and finally a shot from the opening of Momma cooking in the kitchen. In the tumult of images there's a seeming chaos befitting J.R.'s emotional state. Nevertheless, one can see his divided sexuality in its purest form. He's reached a point in which fundamental change may be possible. Religion in the form of the confessional has enabled him to confront himself. He's not so much committing his soul to Christ as he's beginning to experience his inner chaos in an unavoidable way. J.R.'s crisis can't be separated from his religious upbringing. The exaltation of the Virgin Mary, of the mother who cooks and serves, and of virginity have helped to get him into this fix. (It's interesting to note here that the Virgin Mary is more prominent in the final sequence than Christ.) The confessional can help to get him out of it. It's bound to be a violent, soul-wrenching process, however. Will the violence be externalized and acted out against others, or resolved by self-examination? J.R.'s religious training will provide the answer as we see in this final sequence. The coda-like ending of rage, destruction, and potential regeneration will be repeated with greater skill in *Taxi Driver*, *Raging Bull*, *Life Lessons,* and other films. It's another and probably the most important signature element.

In the final shot of the film Joey says "see ya tomorrow" to J.R. His life will go on as before but with a difference.

Boxcar Bertha

Despite the freshness and originality of *Who's That Knocking at My Door?*
the film was a commercial failure—even with the addition of the extended
sex sequence. Scorsese then worked as assistant director and editor on the
documentary *Woodstock* (1970) but he was no closer to success. A chance
to work for Roger Corman, the exploitation film producer, presented itself
and Scorsese jumped at the chance, realizing he could begin to establish
himself as a money-making director. *Boxcar Bertha* was to be a sequel to
Corman's *Bloody Mama* and freely based on the Bertha Thompson
autobiography, *Sister of the Road*, which Julie Corman had discovered and
pressed on her husband. Corman was unabashed at doing a *Bonnie and
Clyde* knock-off. "It's *Bonnie and Clyde* we're doing," he told Scorsese.[8]
The film was to have a tight, nonextendable shooting schedule of twenty-
four days, rigid budget, plenty of violence, mild sex, car chases, train and
bank robberies. Scorsese may have winced at the manufactured nature of
the script but he knew Corman's reputation for giving young directors
their first big break (Coppola, Bogdanovich, and Demme among others at
one time or another). The violence in *Boxcar Bertha* is the most gratuitous
in Scorsese's work, something like the violence in *Cape Fear*. When he

showed John Cassavetes the rough cut, Cassavetes pronounced it "a piece of shit" and told Scorsese not to get trapped in exploitation films.[9] But *Boxcar Bertha* is hardly a piece of shit; it's a carefully made film in which Scorsese storyboarded every shot. He knew he had to work fast to come in under budget and shooting schedule.

Another attraction to the project was Corman's willingness to give his directors freedom as long as the requisite scenes of sex and violence were depicted. Scorsese was thus able to turn the story of Bertha Thompson into a religious drama in which Bertha becomes the fallen woman who worships the Christ-like union organizer Big Bill Shelly. *Boxcar Bertha* is a kind of rehearsal for *The Last Temptation of Christ*. The Kazantzakis novel of the same name is a shadow text to the film, for Barbara Hershey and David Carradine, the major stars, gave Scorsese the novel during production and Hershey asked him to reserve the role of Mary Magdalene for her if he ever made a film adaptation.

Corman liked to think his films had somewhat hidden social and political messages of a liberal persuasion, but *Boxcar Bertha* is hardly subtle in its depiction of the downtrodden working man and the capitalist exploiter and his goons, as well as the racist attitudes of southern sheriffs and the local populace. Big Bill Shelly (Carradine) as an idealistic union organizer who is persecuted by the brutal railroad owner (played by his father, John Carradine) as well as by the local authorities who see him as a "nigger lover" because of his friendship with the harmonica playing Von Morton. But Big Bill increasingly compromises himself by continuing to rob banks in order to support himself and his lover Bertha (Hershey) and their friend the cardsharp Rake Brown. Bill's group is thus hardly a collection of virtuous disciples; Bertha is a part-time prostitute who has murdered a man in a gambling argument ignited by Rake's cheating. You would imagine her to be a fairly hardened character but as played by Barbara Hershey she's pretty, fresh, with a dazzling smile. She also wears a collection of fetching hats. Her role is a tip-off—if one were needed—that the film is more an entertainment than serious social commentary. It lacks the passages of bleak poverty that gave weight to *Bonnie and Clyde*. Bill's gang has fun stealing trains and running them through the country-side with whistle blowing, escaping from chain gangs, engaging in car chases, robbing banks. The celebration of the rebel outsider is the serious business of the film and doesn't entirely blend with Scorsese's attempt to turn the action into a religious parable. One could argue that Bill is a popularized version of the political saint—an idealist who refuses to back away from a corrupt world and who risks his own corruption in so doing—but his enthusiastic participation on the robberies (in spite of later regrets) invalidates this view. He's more like J.R. in *Mean Streets* than the Christ of *Last Temptation*.

The sequential, road-movie structure of *Sister of the Road* seems at first glance to operate in a desultory way in the film. In fact the whole thrust of the action builds toward the violent ending. *Boxcar Bertha* is the first Scorsese film to establish a structure which will occur again and again—in *Mean Streets*, *Taxi Driver*, *The Last Temptation*, *Cape Fear*, *Bringing Out the Dead*. The violent endings in these films usually issue in some form of purgation if not transcendence. But this does not happen in *Boxcar Bertha*.

Bertha seems a sweet, happy-go-lucky tramp whose only dedication is to Bill. It's he who undergoes the greatest transformation. His life at first seems somewhat aimless, hopping freights here and there and attempting to organize the railroad workers when he can. A series of savage beatings by railroad cops, local sheriffs, chain gang wardens (all rendered in graphic detail) makes him more and more desperate. When he begins to rob banks it's as if he's given up on union organizing and is trying to get the easiest payback he can from capitalist bosses. Learning that he's described in the press as a common crook, he moves to leave the gang and a brief sequence of shots gives us a passage which anticipates Scorsese's later skill. The sequence occurs in a slatted corridor, light coming in from the side as Bill moves toward the camera. Scorsese may be influenced here by Welles' use of slatted walls and harsh sidelight in K's visit to the artist in *The Trial*. There are two fast zooms emphasizing the depth of the corridor and several quick cuts to suggest Bill's agitated movement and the others' equally agitated vocal pleas to persuade him not to leave. The darkness of the images, punctuated with bursts of light, powerfully suggests Bill's fateful decision. This is the first of many eloquent corridor shots in Scorsese's films (perhaps the greatest being the hallway and stairwell shots at the end of *Taxi Driver*). He's our finest poet of confined spaces.

From here to the end Bill seems to submit to his fate. A union leader refuses his offer of $3000, his share of the train robbery ("all you socialist bastards are just alike"). He's perceived as a "red," an unpatriotic destroyer of the system. He doesn't have the intellectual resources to preserve himself by political reasoning in the face of such misunderstanding (nor would Corman be interested in such a story). The low point of his progress (he might regard it as a high point) occurs when he and Bertha and his group rob the guests at a fancy dress party given by the head of the railroad. Bertha, wearing an ill-fitting plush dress, adorns herself with the stolen jewelry in front of the guests. Again he's called a common criminal by the big boss and his reply as he gives the boss back his watch is "I don't want your watch. I just want to smash your railroad." It's a brave statement accompanying an ineffectual, absurd act. Two black-dressed goons burst in at this point and kill one of Bill's group, the cardsharp Rake Brown. Bill is brutally beaten once more.

These goons are, for some reason, decked out like Laurel and Hardy—the bigger, fatter one sporting a small moustache and both wearing bowler hats. But they're decidedly unfunny, dealing out awful violence whenever they mysteriously appear. No effort is ever made to account for their sudden appearances. They're like the old furies of classic drama, showing up out of the blue. Scorsese evidently saw them, in part, as comedians. Like Hershey's innocent, sweet Bertha and much of the graphic violence, we're meant to see them as figures of fun as much as threat. There's little realism here, except in Scorsese's excellent use of folk music. Von Morton's blues harmonica and the various episodes accompanied by blues guitar and singer, especially in the sequence where Bill's gang hangs out in a country church, give the film some authenticity.

The violent ending of the film is Scorsese's tour de force. Bill's crucifixion is really three acts in one tumultuous fifty-eight shot sequence: the crucifixion itself, Von Morton's revenge, the final separation of Bill from Bertha. In *Scorsese on Scorsese*, the filmmaker says, "I had nothing to do with the final scene in which the main character was crucified. It was in the script that was given to me, and I thought it was a sign from God."[10] This comment doesn't acknowledge the masterful way Scorsese made the ending his own, though it does suggest the religious passion that went into the making—of the ending at least, if not the whole film.

The sequence begins with an arresting shot from behind a freight car door as Bill's hand is nailed to the wood. We see his fingers only as they jerk in response to the sound of hammering, and we see the nails coming through the wood. We don't see his flesh pierced or see any blood, but our imaginations provide the images even more powerfully because they are not seen. This image is repeated in shot 51, toward the end of the film, as the train moves away from Bertha. In shot 5 we have an overhead shot straight down on Bill as he cries in anguish and passes out. This overhead angle may have been influenced by Dali's painting of the crucifixion. In 8 one of the thugs nails a small torn white piece of paper above Bill's head. Bertha who was passed out on the ground has been watching. In shot 13 Von Morton's revenge begins as he cooly employs a pump action shotgun to kill the thugs one by one. From 13 to 44 we have a somewhat repetitive pattern of fast shots in which we see a close-up of Von's hands as he pumps the gun, a close-up of the smoking muzzle of the gun, a thug receiving the blast, usually in the chest, a shot of the thug falling back, a shot of the thug hitting the ground. The revenge sequence slows noticeably when Von kills the Laurel and Hardy goons. One in particular is wounded and then dispatched after crawling along the ground. He rolls over on his back with his mouth open in an almost leisurely manner. In shot 45 the third part of the sequence begins with an establishing shot of the whole scene of carnage as Von walks toward Bertha and lifts her up. As the train begins to move away in 51 we have a downshot of Bill as Bertha moves toward him. The remaining shots show Bertha running after Bill as the train rises up an embankment away from her. The note here is one of separation as much as transcendence. Bill remains a fully flawed human being more than a spiritual embodiment of the Christ figure. His crucifixion is a dry run for the great crucifixion episode in *Last Temptation.*

The ending of *Boxcar Bertha* is Scorsese's first full-blown evocation of the mixture of violence and religion, an area of experience he'll explore in many of his later films. The amalgam of goodness and criminality in Bill is crudely joined. He doesn't really resolve his contradictions or come to any spiritual awakening, much less transcendence. Had Scorsese had more control over the script, these elements would have been more fully resolved. Nevertheless, the film demonstrates—particularly in its ending— the ability of a young director to produce good work under strictures not his own.

Notes

1. *Scorsese on Scorsese* (London: Faber and Faber, 1989), 3.
2. Ibid., 3.
3. Ibid., 12.
4. Ibid., 15.
5. Ibid., 15.
6. Les Keyser, *Martin Scorsese* (New York: Twayne Publishing Co., 1992), 24.
7. *Scorsese on Scorsese*, 28.
8. Ibid., 36.
9. Ibid., 38.
10. Ibid., 36.

Chapter 2

A NEW VOICE

MEAN STREETS, 1973
ITALIANAMERICAN, 1974

Mean Streets

It's hard to overstate the importance of *Mean Streets*. Having served his apprenticeship in his film school work and with Roger Corman, Scorsese had the freedom to make his own statement. Pauline Kael's tireless efforts in the *New Yorker* probably prevented the film's early disappearance and gave him the boost he needed.

The film establishes Scorsese's basic subject matter: urban violence, gang behavior, and the guilt and suffering that flow from it. The two central characters, Charlie (Harvey Keitel) and Johnny Boy (Robert De Niro), are benchmark figures who reappear in later films. Charlie, the conscience stricken mediator, is repeated in Henry Hill (Ray Liotta) in *Goodfellas*, Joey LaMotta (Joe Pesci) in *Raging Bull*, and Ace Rothstein (De Niro) in *Casino*. Johnny Boy the outlaw sociopath is reenacted in a whole slew of De Niro roles: Travis Bickle in *Taxi Driver*, Jake LaMotta in *Raging Bull*, Max Cody in *Cape Fear*, and Rupert Pupkin in *King of Comedy*, as well as two Joe Pesci roles: Tommy de Vito (*Goodfellas*) and Nicky Santoro (*Casino*). One can even argue that the repressed Newland Archer (Daniel Day-Lewis) and the sophisticated Ellen Olenska (Michelle Pfeiffer) in *The Age of Innocence* play out variations of this opposition. In *Mean Streets* Scorsese discovers the essential drama of the opposed selves he'll use in many later films. Other essential elements are laid down as well: the use of popular music from the period to accompany specific shots and sequences, and even basic shot procedure such as the use of tracking shots to introduce the patrons of Tony's bar, and following shots of a central character (Charlie) as he enters the bar. These shots are used in later films—most particularly in *Goodfellas*. Another element of Scorsese's method is explored fully: the use of improvisation between actors in certain crucial encounters. *Mean Streets* establishes Scorsese's basic subject matter and his cinematic procedure as well. In this respect the film can be seen as a continuation of the equally important *Who's That Knocking*. Charlie continues J.R.'s problematic situation in the earlier film: his conflicted sexual relation with Teresa, another good girl like "the girl" in *Knocking*, whose damaged condition poses a threat to his desire for purity in a lover; his allegiance to the guys, over and above his devotion to Teresa, which keeps him in a state of protracted adolescence; his desire to play a mediating role between the often wild and violent behavior of his friends and their potential victims—in other words to have it both ways as saint and sinner. This conflict is sharpened in *Mean Streets*. Charlie is older, more aware of spiritual contradictions, but still unable to resolve them. *Mean Streets* may be a much more professional product—in acting, editing, soundtrack, cinematography—but its origins and basic concerns lie in *Who's That Knocking*.

Like the later *Goodfellas*, the film attempts to depict mob behavior in a realistic, unromanticized way. Early passages in the film especially have a documentary quality—like Michael's theft of a truckload of German camera lenses under the elevated subway (they turn out to be unusable

Japanese adapters). The use of hand-held camera and steadycam shots in the streets gives a gritty sense of actuality. This feeling is enhanced by the use of home movie footage of the leading characters in the beginning, which then flows into documentary sequences of the feast of San Gennaro in the New York section of Little Italy, the celebration that forms the backdrop to the film's drama.

The main characters are introduced with great economy. They're a kind of junior mafia of small time street hustlers and layabouts. Scorsese seems to have been thinking of Fellini's *Vitelloni* and its comic treatment of indigent young men as much as the violence and religion of Visconti's *Rocco and His Brothers*. We see Tony kick a drug addict out of his bar; Michael tries to sell his lenses without knowing what they really are; Johnny Boy blows up a mail box in a burst of juvenile energy. The longest introduction is given to Charlie, the film's central character, as he kneels in church. His inner dialogue is presented in two voices: a high-pitched voice which condemns the priestly rigmarole of automatic penance and a lower, calmer voice in which he rejects the idea of doing his own penance without help and speaks of the pain of spiritual suffering. He's a divided character: a would-be priest who wants to work out his salvation in the streets. In the opening of the film, while the screen is dark, we hear his voice saying, "You don't make up for your sins in church, you do it in the streets. You do it at home. The rest is bullshit and you know it." Immediately after the church sequence the camera follows Charlie into Tony's as he dances his way along the bar, greeting friends, moving up onto the stage where he removes his coat and dances with a nearly nude black dancer. He's Mr. Cool, the ultimate performer—both in church and in the bar. Chosen by the local godfather to be his debt collector, Charlie has a significant role in the community. He has the power, he believes, to do good within the system. But it's a closed system, both geographically in its confinement to the few blocks of Little Italy and culturally in its confinement to the rigid and often violent code of the local mafia. Charlie can't imagine himself outside this life; it's a given and he must live it. He wants to be a secular priest and he wants to make money in the system. In other words, he wants to have it both ways. He's aware of the split and often performs parodies of priestly rituals such as blessing the drinks at the bar, making the sign of the cross to his friends. These antics are both joking (as a kind of self mockery) and serious. As a result Charlie is often razzed as a phoney "St. Charles" and his lover Teresa laughs at him when he says, "Lord, I'm trying." His habit of putting his hand in any flame which presents itself has an element of self-dramatization as well as religious purgation. The godfather's warning to Charlie to stay away from Teresa and Johnny Boy, Charlie's closest friends, because they are mentally unbalanced (Teresa is an epileptic) is given added weight because he's promised to turn over a restaurant to him. But Charlie can't turn his back on them. He attempts to hide these relationships from the godfather just as he attempts to negotiate his own penance with God. Each relationship assuages his guilt and is an attempt to work out his own salvation—"in the streets" with Johnny Boy and "at home" with Teresa. Like the young Scorsese he wants to be both priest and tough guy. Salvation in the streets with Johnny Boy inevitably involves violence and the guilt that goes with it. The violence in Charlie is internal as he struggles in the early church sequence to resolve his turmoil.

The relationship with Teresa is fairly straight-forward. He loves her and wants to do good by taking care of her. He also half-jokingly calls her a cunt. He's full of the macho attitude of the street gang: women come second, or even third, after male allegiance. He's more turned on by the black dancer and even sets up a date with her and then backs off, presumably in fear of what the godfather will think. His self-division includes the good girl-bad girl split. One reason he can't give Teresa up is that she embodies that idealism in him which he mocks when he's around the guys. Still, she isn't as self-effacing and compliant as "the girl" in *Knocking*. She's an advance in Scorsese's depiction of women.

Charlie's connection to Johnny Boy is more complex. On the surface, it doesn't make any sense. Johnny Boy's recklessness and self-destructiveness is everything Charlie should avoid if he wants to succeed with the godfather whose basic strategy is to maintain order and control. Charlie's friends are always asking him why he continues to help Johnny Boy. A brief incident later in the film gives us one answer. As they walk along the street Charlie tells him that he never recovered from a beating the cops gave him and Johnny Boy's reply is that Charlie took off and left him to occupy the cops. This statement is made matter-of-factly, without much accusation. Immediately afterward the two engage in a play fight with trash can lids. Charlie, we are to understand from this, feels guilt for the brain damage Johnny Boy suffered while he ran away. They're old friends who grew up together in the streets and Charlie is well aware of what Johnny Boy was like before the beating. Charlie has an essential decency despite his role-playing and self-delusion.

Charlie can feel closer to God by helping Johnny Boy. He calls him his penance when he sees him enter Tony's bar. The sequence is presented in slow motion as Johnny Boy moves down the bar toward Charlie (a reverse of Charlie's entrance) who turns away before he eventually embraces his friend. Charlie's ambivalence is nicely evoked here. He doesn't want to see Johnny Boy yet he covers up this instinctive reaction very successfully—to himself as well as the others. He's a bit repressed, a bit masked. The out-of-control Johnny Boy is an appealing threat to him. He can act out the aggression Charlie keeps under control. This aggression on Charlie's part is best seen in a strange incident in which Charlie comes on forcefully to a woman at the bar who is having a fight with her friend. This is Charlie the tough guy. He challenges the friend to a fight and, with Johnny Boy's help, roughs him up. It's an action one might expect from Johnny Boy, except that he rarely shows interest in women. Johnny Boy's entrance to the bar is even more stylized than Charlie's. He checks his pants rather than his overcoat, jiving all the time to the soundtrack's accompaniment of the rock music which is usually associated with him, chewing gum and giving off a constant patter. There's a doubleness here: his electric craziness overlaid with Charlie's vision of him as his cross to bear. "Thanks a lot Lord," Charlie says inwardly as he sees Johnny Boy, "we play by your rules don't we?" This is the big question Charlie doesn't want to face since he wants to play by his own rules.

If *Mean Streets* can be said to have a plot, it involves Charlie's attempts to get Johnny Boy to pay his heavy debts and thus to keep him from further injury as well as to keep himself in the good graces of the godfather. Most of the film involves episodes from the street life of Charlie and his friends and are shot in an informal documentary style: Michael's rip off of two kids who want to buy fireworks, Charlie's attempts to collect money from fat Joey in a pool hall as well as from Oscar the failing owner of the restaurant Charlie is likely to inherit, the killing of a drunk in Tony's bar by a young hood who wants to prove his usefulness to the godfather, the wild eruption of a Vietnam veteran in the bar. There's a curious unreality to the fight in fat Joey's poolroom, which occurs in two phases. In the first the fight is wild and savage with Johnny Boy striking out with a pool cue, people battering each other. Nobody seems bloodied or even bruised and their clothes seem barely disarranged when the cops show up and receive their bribes. The resumption of the fight is pure Keystone Kops with Joey and his pals falling down *en masse* as Charlie and the others scamper up the stairs. These incidents, most of them violent, are preparations for the horrific sequence which ends the film.

The core of the film is Charlie's relationship with Johnny Boy and its dynamics are first seen in a long sequence immediately after Johnny Boy enters the bar and produces money for drinks. In a storeroom off the bar where Charlie has dragged him we watch Johnny Boy manipulate Charlie by telling him a series of stories about how he's really been paying his debts. Charlie clearly doesn't believe him but allows himself to be persuaded by his friend's playfulness and neediness. His role is like the godfather's except that he's incapable of taking a firm position. The sequence lasts four minutes and fifty-five seconds and is the first good example of Scorsese's use of improvisation in *Mean Streets*. De Niro's Johnny Boy is full of body gestures and effusive language while Charlie prods him to discard one story after another. We're given a series of shot/reverse shots with a few medium shots thrown in for variation. It's clearly an improvised sequence and it goes on too long. We could get the same understanding at half the length. There's a natural, spontaneous flow which is almost impossible to edit. Its looseness stands in sharp contrast to the economy of the introductions of the main characters. This emphasis on improvisation is a strength, but also a weakness, particularly when it goes out of control in *New York, New York*. It should be added that other exchanges which have an improvised feeling like Charlie and Teresa in bed, or at the beach, or Johnny Boy's vicious attack on Charlie and Teresa ("what happens when she comes?") are kept to a minimum.

Charlie and Johnny Boy are both using each other: Charlie needs Johnny Boy for his compromised religious quest, and because Johnny Boy acts out the tough guy enclosed in Charlie. Johnny Boy needs Charlie for protection from his increasingly angry creditors, especially Michael. Tony's only eruption involves stinging criticism of each one. He tells Charlie he's a fool not to be more cynical about the church—that it's a business organization like any other. He calls Johnny Boy a "scumbag" and Charlie has to perform his habitual role of breaking up the fight that ensues. Tony is the only character in the film who has an unadulterated love for another creature, a young lion which he embraces inside the cage in his storeroom, while the other characters look on in awe and fear.

Charlie's relationship with Teresa is heavily voyeuristic. His apartment window looks into hers, where she unaccountably undresses without pulling the curtain. When she gets angry at being called a cunt and goes nude to the window Charlie tells her to move because "someone might see you." Teresa then tells him to cover his eyes while she dresses but he peeks through his fingers and Scorsese gives us shots of her body through the fingers. The objectification of Teresa doesn't diminish Charlie's love for her, but it's a love full of disturbing images as well as tenderness and playfulness (Charlie tells her he has a dream in which he comes blood with her). The objectification keeps her at a safe distance. He may perceive Teresa as more of a threat than Johnny Boy because of their sexual connection. Her threat is twofold: she represents a violation of the godfather's instructions and, even more powerfully, she challenges Charlie to give up his mafia activities, with all their comfortable rituals and confinements, and begin to make a new world for himself. She presents the same difficulty to Charlie as "the girl" does to J.R. in *Who's That Knocking*. She wants to live with him and to move out of Little Italy. The anxiety of this enterprise outweighs even his sexual ambivalence to her damaged psyche. In any case, he's quick to abandon her to the care of a neighbor when she has an epileptic attack in the stairwell after Johnny Boy's verbal assault and quick departure. This attack on Charlie and Teresa reveals Johnny Boy's jealousy over Charlie's good life, particularly as his own life collapses. ("Everybody likes Charlie. He's a fucking politician." "I don't want to break up a happy household.") Charlie's pursuit of Johnny Boy demonstrates the supremacy of the male bond. He needs to save him more than her. He also needs to keep Johnny Boy from making it known to the godfather that he's going against his instructions.

Loosely episodic in its structure, *Mean Streets* moves inevitably toward the sequence of harrowing violence that concludes the film. Michael's attack on Johnny Boy in a car chase is accompanied by the screaming guitars of a rock band as well as the screams of the wounded. Charlie and Teresa and Johnny Boy are each bloodied by the ensuing car crash as well as the shots from Michael's hired gun (played by Scorsese). It's the kind of raw unglamorized violence that stays in the mind's eye and that becomes a signature of Scorsese's films. We see a series of fast shots in which Johnny Boy is hit in the neck, Charlie in the hand, Johnny Boy hangs out the window screaming as the car careens off two cars before hitting a fire hydrant which erupts in a geyser of water. There's a shot of a bloody hand sticking out of a hole in the fractured windshield before we see firemen and police attending to the victims. The religious subtext to this carnage is indicated by Scorsese kissing the gun before he fires, like the Latino kid kissing his cross before he's attacked in *Who's That Knocking*. Charlie kneels beside the car, his bloody hands clasped before him in a posture resembling suffering and worship. These shots are intercut by shots of the religious and cultural celebration of San Gennaro going on at the same time. This is Charlie's dark night of the soul. It has been coming toward him for a long time and now it has arrived in the form of searing violence. His practices of avoidance are finished. The violence which nearly kills him and Teresa and Johnny Boy will compel a form of awakening on his part—or he will go under. The ending of *Mean Streets* is a prefiguration of the violent ending of *Taxi Driver*, right down to the high shot looking down at the crowd which has formed around the crash. Equally effective are the brief shots of Tony washing his hands, the godfather watching TV, and the black dancer lighting a cigarette in a restaurant. Each is momentarily alone as are Charlie, Teresa, and Johnny Boy as they struggle to survive.

Mean Streets is a film about youth, its excesses, confusions, excitements. Charlie, Johnny Boy, Tony, and Michael may look like men but they're really still boys dressed up in sharp suits. This is made abundantly clear in one of the best shots of the film, Charlie's drunken episode at a party at the bar. In this single shot lasting eighty seconds the camera focuses on Charlie's face as he gets drunker and drunker. The shot is accompanied by a fast-paced nonsense song and by distorted rear projection. Scorsese may have been thinking of the great drunken sequence in Murnau's *The Last Laugh*. At any rate, Charlie's face seems to get more and more boyish and vulnerable as the shot goes along. It's a remarkable compression of time in a single shot. This shot is the best example of Scorsese's use of expressionist distortion in a film largely characterized by documentary realism. It's a preview of the more pervasive distortions in later films like *Taxi Driver*, *Raging Bull*, and *Bringing Out the Dead*. The fact that Charlie and his friends are still partially boys does not make their games any less deadly. It does mean that in Charlie's case, for instance, he doesn't seem to be fully aware of the threat from Michael since he and Teresa and Johnny Boy playfully go to another of their bad movies before they borrow Tony's car to get out of town.

We know Charlie will survive his wounds but we don't know if he'll learn from them. We don't know if he'll become less involved with the macho rituals of the gang, less fixed in the arrested adolescence the gang preserves, less misogynist in his attitudes toward women and open to a mature relationship.

Italianamerican

Italianamerican was made in 1974 funded by a grant from the National Endowment for the Humanities as part of a projected series about immigrants. Having completed *Alice Doesn't Live Here Anymore*, Scorsese wanted to keep busy and vary his production by making a documentary. He regards the film as a counterpart to *Mean Streets* and though it bears little thematic and visual connection to that film (though some of the contemporary street shots are reminiscent of *Mean Streets*) it does concern itself with that confined area of New York known as Little Italy. It will be discussed briefly here.

The forty-five minute documentary, like the later *American Boy*, is essentially an interview in which Scorsese elicits stories of his family's past from his father and mother, Charles and Catherine. It was edited down from about five-and-a-half hours of continuous footage shot in the living room and kitchen of the parents' small apartment on Elizabeth Street and around the dining room table while the three Scorseses eat a leisurely meal. Scorsese sits mostly out of the frame holding a sheaf of notes (as in *American Boy*) which he uses to give structure to the conversation. A linking device throughout is Catherine's preparation of a tomato-based pasta sauce, the recipe for which is humorously and usefully provided at the end after the credits. The atmosphere is affectionate and lively.

In the first part of the film the senior Scorseses talk about their early life in the city: cramped living space, no electricity, a mixture of mainly Jewish and Italian immigrants on their street. Black and white photos of the family are shown as are shots of a recent trip to Italy. Gradually Scorsese nudges his mom and dad to talk about their parents' life in Sicily and their immigration to the United States. Archival documentary footage of immigrants in the city is used. The weight of the past is tangibly felt in these images and in the stories of the endless workdays of the grandparents, their need to take in boarders, sometimes living twelve in a three-room space with a toilet down the hall or in the backyard of the tenement. There's a vivid and affectionate argument about which family made the best wine. The origins of the Italian immigrant movement are nicely portrayed here.

The emphasis on family life is a major dimension of *Italianamerican*, occurring mainly around cooking and eating. We're reminded of later scenes in *Goodfellas*, the careful food preparation in jail, for instance. Scorsese clearly wanted to make a loving record of his parents' relationship as well as their immigrant past. Catherine at first takes charge of the interview, directing Charles where to sit, but he soon comes forward and more than holds his own, though in a different style. She's the storyteller, the inventor, with her semi-legendary tale of how her mother first saw her father from a low balcony as he rode through town in a military parade, and her fondness for folk tales. One can easily see why her son used her so often in his films. Charles is more factual and down-to-earth—more like a documentary filmmaker. He criticizes her manner right away: "She's trying to put on . . . she should talk natural." This is, in fact, the advice Scorsese gives Stephen Prince at the end of *American Boy*: stop acting, get real. We can see the two sides of Scorsese the filmmaker (and actor) in his parents. As in so many of his films (*Mean Streets, Who's That Knocking, Casino, Raging Bull*) the documentary and the fictional are both present and enhance each other.

Chapter 3

A CAREER CHOICE

ALICE DOESN'T LIVE HERE ANYMORE, 1974

It is interesting to speculate about Scorsese's next choice of projects, after *Mean Streets. Alice Doesn't Live Here Anymore* (1974) seems an odd selection for him. It's a film about women's issues, a road movie, with touches of the soap opera and sitcom, and it was shot in the bright, wide-open spaces of the Southwest—all unusual dimensions for Scorsese. If *Mean Streets* came from his deepest creative energies, *Alice* certainly did not. But *Mean Streets* didn't have much success; and when Ellen Burstyn approached him with the script for *Alice*, it's likely that he felt he could establish himself as a popular director. The film won Burstyn an Oscar for

Best Actress, and it did well at the box office; but though it's a good
enough effort, it's hardly one of Scorsese's best films. Scorsese was a
good choice for Burstyn because he could add realism to a script which,
in the wrong hands, could turn maudlin. Still, it's an example of a flawed
effort which, in its economic success, helped a new director's career
immeasurably.

The film follows Alice and young son, Tommy, as they move from
town to town after the death of her abusive husband. She finds work as a
singer, falls into another abusive relationship, pulls up stakes and hits the
road, finally finding true love and happiness with a handsome, young
rancher whom she meets in a diner where she works as a waitress. The
episodic structure of encounters strung out along the road give the film an
open, Western feeling which is accentuated by Scorsese's images of long,
straight highways, broad, flat vistas in hard, even glaring, light and a series
of nondescript motel settings.

Scorsese's strategy with his subject is evident from the first images.
The credits are shot against a crumpled blue material, while a singer
croons "You'll Never Know Just How Much I Love You." It's a parody
of the older, heartwarming films from the '30s and '40s. Alice's youth is
presented in a brief sequence in which she walks in the country road near
her house in a suffused, rosy light meant to resemble sunset. The
artificiality of the lighting (undoubtedly shot in the studio like the older
films) and the dreamy song quickly give way to loud rock music and an
overhead pan shot in natural light of the bedroom community of Socorro,
New Mexico, where Alice lives now. A gritty, suburban present replaces
a sentimentalized rural past.

Alice is a placater. Her husband, Donald, is taciturn and undemonstra-
tive in his affections and angry at her and Tommy. Alice's response is to
try and please him with a special dinner. Her passivity is partially based
on her economic dependence; she has no special skills other than once
having been a singer. The script gets rid of Donald fast in a car accident,
and Alice is on her own. She's feisty but uncertain of herself. She tells her
best friend that she could live without a man, but immediately falls into a
relationship with Ben (Harvey Keitel), a younger man who is attracted to
her singing at a bar in a new town where she's resolutely managed to get
a job. The sequences of her search for a singing job nicely suggest both
her stubbornness and her vulnerability. Oddly enough, her singing is more
relaxed and natural when she practices on the piano at home than in the
bar, where she assumes a coquettish inflection. She appears to know what
the customers, mainly men, want and her desire to be a pleaser assists her.
Ben picks up on this not-so-hidden signal and pursues her. He's fresh and

charming in the wooing posture, but turns into a monster when he catches his wife in an emotional visit to Alice. The abusive male in Donald is intensified in Ben. He breaks down the door, kicks his wife around the floor and pulls a knife on her, and then makes Alice promise to meet him for a date later that day, before he goes out the door combing his hair. Harvey Keitel's powerful performance suggests that he is two different people, in much the same way women perceive the two sides of abusers: winning and apologetic one moment, raging the next.

Alice is not an idealized figure and neither is Tommy. He's a ten-year-old brat, both indulged and neglected—indulged because he is neglected. Alice often leaves him alone in their motel room where he watches TV and gets grouchy. In a sly cinematic reference, he watches Betty Grable have her clothes torn by a man and then begin singing, "Cuddle up a little closer." Scorsese always has an appropriate movie quote handy. No wonder Tommy is a "smart-ass kid": he's mad at his mom for leaving him alone, and then she can't do enough for him to make up for it. Alice herself isn't the most thoughtful mother; she doesn't provide Tommy with books or toys to help him on the road or in the motel. She loves him but she's very preoccupied about their economic fate. It's the daffy waitress, Vera, who gives Tommy a book to read and color.

The diner sequences are some of the weakest in the movie. Scorsese wants to suggest the pressure Alice works under so he keys up the sound and works the camera around energetically to create a frenzied atmosphere. This environment is a test Alice must pass if she's to succeed. The fry cook, Mel (played by Vic Tayback), adds a sitcom element, as does Valerie Curtin as Vera. It's a bit like a *Cheers* version of Mel's Diner. Alice's bonding with the salty-mouthed waitress, Flo (Diane Ladd), brings the women's issue forward. Her initial dislike of Flo dissolves in a key scene in which she's both horrified/embarrassed and amused when Flo announces to the customers that Alice has been out in back "taking a shit." It's a tricky scene and doesn't quite work, though Burstyn's reaction is full of complex emotions. As Alice, Flo, and Vera embrace, we're asked to believe that Alice has switched from outrage to acceptance. Flo's unconditional support of Alice from then on helps pull her through.

The presence of Kris Kristofferson as David, Alice's final lover, is more problematic. He's a good eight to ten years younger than Alice and is very handsome and charismatic. He also has a big ranch and horses which he rides with Tommy. He's like a figure from Alice's fantasy, a dream lover. Presumably he's attracted to Alice because he's lonely: his wife left with their two kids, and Alice can provide a ready-made family. Why he's lonely isn't clear; he lives on the outskirts of Tucson, though the film never gives a feeling of a big city which would have lots of attractive women his age. It's like a rural environment. The improvised scenes of affection between David and Alice have a very natural feeling, however. The test in their relationship occurs when Tommy insults and hits David and David strikes back, knocking Tommy down. Like Ben, he pursues Alice by coming to the diner and asking for a reconciliation. Unlike Ben, he says he's willing to give up his ranch and go with her to California as she'd planned. He's too selfless here (too much the opposite of Ben), and his long, angry, affectionate exchange with Alice in front of the customers as they reconcile doesn't work very well. It's like a contrived performance within the contrived performance of the film. Though it's a woman's movie, Lawrence Friedman is perceptive in noting that it "militates against feminist assertion."[1] Alice is most fulfilled when there's a male presence in her life, whether it's her son whose presence dictates many of her decisions—or a suitor.

One wonders how much control Scorsese had over the script. There are two major lapses which could have been cut: the first is the longish lyrics to a song the bar owner recites to Alice before he eventually hires her. He wants her to sing this song about "what's the use of getting married," but Alice doesn't know it. It is supposed to be funny but is not. The second is a very long exchange in which Tommy tries to explain a joke about a gorilla to Alice as they drive along. He goes through the joke once in an elaborate and confusing way, and then when she doesn't get it, he begins again. Probably this overly cute exchange was improvised; it certainly needed to be pared down.

As a whole, the film doesn't have much of Scorsese's personal imprint. Like *Boxcar Bertha* and the later *The Color of Money* and *Cape Fear*, it's an attempt to prove to the industry—and the investors who fund it—that he can do work that sells. Its success at the box office and at the Academy Awards gave Scorsese the opportunity to do his best work. In visual terms *Alice* isn't up to his later standards, though there's one brief sequence that sticks. Alice and Flo are sitting outside, in back of the diner, chatting quietly, leaning back, the sun in their faces. Scorsese uses a tight shot from one side, then the other side, presenting their faces in profile. They look like sisters, even twins. In the next shot we see them from a far distance as the camera looks down the empty dirt street. It's the establishing shot that could have come first in the usual grammar of film. The camera holds several beats and a gust of wind blows a thin cloud of dust toward them under a brilliant blue sky. It's a hard, bright, barren setting where you're lucky if you can find friendship and love.

Note

1. Lawrence Friedman, *The Cinema of Martin Scorsese* (New York: Continuum Publishing Co., 1998), 55.

Chapter 4

THE STRANGE AND FAMILIAR

TAXI DRIVER, 1976

Paul Schrader has said he wrote the script for *Taxi Driver* in ten days, and that it came out of him like an explosion. Disaffected from his Midwest upbringing in the Christian Reformed Church, a stern Calvinist offshoot, he had at one point been living in his car and wondering if he'd survive. The film has a feeling of bottled-up rage and hopelessness. In Scorsese and De Niro, Schrader found the perfect artists to render his apocalyptic vision of a diseased world. Scorsese's first major film, *Taxi Driver* is one of the authentic American masterpieces from the 1970s.

Travis Bickle, the main character, is a kind of undergroundling. Cruising the streets in his taxi, he becomes obsessed with the "vermin" which surround him. He sees Betsy, a pretty woman who works in the campaign of a presidential candidate, and falls for her. She is pure and incorruptible in his mind, far above the sordidness of his usual work life. After he persuades her to go out on a date, she rejects him. As his isolation deepens, he tries to tell a fellow cabby about the sick ideas that keep coming into his head, but the cabby fails to understand. He buys several handguns and prepares for some sort of confrontation. He begins to show up at rallies for the presidential candidate. He happens to encounter a black man robbing the owner at his local grocery store and shoots him. A few days later he tries to persuade a young prostitute to leave her trade. He makes an attempt on the presidential candidate's life without getting off a shot. He then confronts the young prostitute's pimp and shoots him and two other men involved in the prostitution network in a scene of horrifying violence. After he recovers from his own severe gunshot wounds, he is portrayed in the press as a hero.

This brief summary barely suggests the sense of intensifying and inevitable violence which pervades the film. Travis is a time bomb, but he's also oddly ordinary. He is both square and strange. He's the man about whom the neighbors might say, "I didn't think he could do such a thing." True, he keeps to himself and often seems preoccupied, but he also writes his parents loving letters, has a strong—even compulsive—work ethic, means to do good in the world, and has a kind of naïve, even righteous outlook. Like many thoughtful people, he keeps a diary, which Schrader and Scorsese use to great advantage. On the surface, he could be taken for a member of the "moral majority" or a follower of one of our current moral conservatives. There are many such, and they aren't violent. He sees himself as normal. He is one of us, but with a difference. Schrader's point is astute: our criminal excesses grow out of our normality.

The first scene of the film, when he applies for a job as a cabby, is designed to tell us a lot about him in a short space. He implies to the hiring boss that he's a high school dropout, that he likes working at night because he can't sleep, and that he's willing to go "anywhere anytime" with his fares—even into Harlem or the Bronx in the dead of night. The implication here is that his nerves are on edge and he's potentially self-destructive. When asked if his driving record is clean, he says jokingly, "Yeah, it's clean . . . like my conscience." Yet a moment later he doesn't seem to know what moonlighting means when he's asked if he has another job. He's a mixture of the wisecracker and the naïf. His joke about his conscience is really a serious comment, for he wishes his conscience (or, at least, his consciousness) were clean. In fact, it becomes infected as he cruises the neon-lit streets peopled with whores, pimps, dope dealers, and other lowlifes. He comes to wish that a flood would wash all this "scum" away from the streets. This growing monomania makes him the frenzied killer he becomes at the end of the movie. The film as a whole is designed to carefully chart his growing obsession.

Side by side with Travis' deepening alienation, his strangeness, is his desire for a normal, conventional life. When he writes a letter to his parents, he tells them he's doing secret work for the government and planning marriage to the upper-class woman, Betsy (Cybill Shepherd), who has, by this time, rejected him. The letter is not so much a lie as a despairing fantasy of the life he wishes he were leading. It's written inside a greeting card which has a picture of two oldsters dressed up as boy scouts, with the caption, "To a Couple of Good Old Scouts." He still holds his parents in affection and probably reveres the life they have together. His squareness and his sickness go together. There's a simplicity here that suggests that Travis hasn't really grown up. His attachment to his parents may be that of a child who still wants to please.

He sees only vileness in the streets, and he sees it through the lens of a radically distorted idealism. Scorsese's camera, it must be added, accentuates the vileness; there is little of the healthy and life-enhancing going on, which Travis would fail to notice. As the camera glances out the window of his taxi, there are always whores, pimps, and junkies in the garish streets. This is an early tip-off that what looks like documentary images of the street à la *Who's That Knocking* and *Mean Streets* is really a visual form of subjective distortion. Scorsese is using the camera in a new way as a means of accentuating Travis' inner state. We haven't seen passages of what could be called subjective expressionism in the earlier films.

Betsy senses the trouble within Travis when she calls him a "walking contradiction"; she's flattered by the intensity of his interest in her but disconcerted by the fanaticism which emerges from underneath his neat, clean and respectful posture. Sport (Harvey Keitel) goes even further. When Travis tells him he knows what's going on, Sport laughs in his face and tells him, "You sure don't look like you do." He has an instinctive sense of Travis' naïveté. De Niro's body language is particularly effective here. There's so much tension in Travis' body waiting to burst out—particularly in the shoulders and neck. While Sport swivels and jives, Travis stands rigid, as if he's partially paralyzed, turning his whole upper body when he wants to move his head to one side.

Travis is unaware of these inner tensions at first. In an early scene with his fellow cabbies, he fails to acknowledge a question from the leader of the group, Wizzard (Peter Boyle). He's distracted by the menacing-looking, fancy-dressed black dudes in the coffee shop. He pops an Alka-Seltzer in a glass and the camera slowly moves down into an extreme close-up of the fizzing and "boiling" water (the camera actually appears to dive into the water). His paranoia (the blacks in the shop) is mixed with a kind of trance-like unfocusedness. The close-up of the Alka-Seltzer is not a point-of-view shot. Travis isn't slowly lowering his face into the stirring water. It's an "inside" shot depicting his inner state (the low-angled tracking shot of the blacks is, as well). It's similar to another effective shot in which Travis phones Betsy after she's rejected him, and the camera moves to the right and holds on an empty hallway. In the first shot he's depressed, withdrawn. The active seething of the Alka-Seltzer is a good image of his own turmoil, which is as yet not fully acknowledged and ready to be acted out. It's another example of subjective expressionism. Schrader's script merely reads "Travis drops two Alka-Seltzers into a glass of water."[1] Scorsese's visual imagination seized on this commonplace detail and transformed it. The empty hallway is a good image of his desolation.[2] Betsy's rejection tips him over the edge into the gun-buying and murderous rage.

From the first shot of the film, behind the credits, of the taxi emerging from the steam rising from the night street, the reality of life inside the taxi and outside on the streets is firmly established. In a quick montage we see rain on the windshield, the gleaming yellow surfaces of the taxi reflected in the bright neon lights, shots of Travis' darting eyes in the mirror, the streets of Times Square and 42nd Street crowded with hookers, lovers, men moving under the marquees of the porno theaters. Scorsese moves us back and forth from the streets to the interior of the taxi, where we watch Travis scanning the street or depositing his money in a wooden cigar box. This life is lurid, potentially dangerous, depressing but real. By contrast, the campaign headquarters where Betsy and her friend, Tom (Albert Brooks), work seems artificial and contrived. The red and white decor, the campaign signs and slogans have an unreal quality. Betsy and Tom, themselves, are role-players; their flirtations are masked by supercilious wittiness and a kind of forced gaiety. They are bright young college graduates who feel they are at the center of power. They carry themselves with a sense of self-importance, which issues in lightly snide and cynical comments such as that selling politics is "like selling mouthwash." Their candidate, Charles Palantine, is a media star, good looking on TV, practiced at voicing palatable phrases which say nothing ("We are the people").

Travis' attempted killing of Palantine isn't a political act. He has no political ideas. When Palantine accidentally takes a ride in his cab and asks him what he'd do to improve the city, he can only rant about the scum in the streets. Palantine then says he's learned more from talking to cabbies than from any of the limo rides he's taken. He may actually believe that he gets in touch with the common man by riding in taxis (taking Travis for the ordinary, the normal), but his whole campaign is presented as a fraudulent manipulation. He's being sold to the public like mouthwash, as Betsy remarks. His words and gestures at the rally are canned, stiff, overrehearsed. He speaks about "We, the People," but it is clear he's no populist. His name, which refers to the hill in Rome where the wealthiest people lived during the empire, suggests where he is really coming from. Schrader is dead-on about the deep cynicism that lies behind politicians' blandishments. He wants us to see through Palantine, whereas Travis cannot; he wants us to be angry, but not in Travis' way, which isn't really directed at Palantine or the system, but at Betsy.

Betsy's privileged and smug world is seen by Travis as higher and purer than his own. ("They cannot touch her.") For her, he is of interest because he comes from below; he is of the people. The coffee shop scene between them is worth looking at fairly closely. It begins with De Niro speaking the words from Travis' diary (the diary is used effectively throughout as a linking device between scenes and as a way into Travis' mind) as they walk toward the coffee shop. Travis' recitation of exactly what each one ate and drank is both simple and touching; this is a big moment in his life.

Travis clumsily tries to make a joke about needing to get "organized," but after explaining clearly what he means, she takes it away from him by saying, "Oh, you mean *organizized.*" He is only momentarily fazed, and proceeds to tell her how strong a connection exists between them. He is projecting his own strong feelings onto her, as he did in the prior scene at her desk when he urgently tells her how lonely and meaningless her life is. She acknowledges a sense of connection to him in a careful way, entirely without affect ("I wouldn't be here if I didn't [feel connected]"). She's curious about this strange, intense man, while he's sure he knows who she is. The scene serves well to reveal how self-enclosed Travis is, how unable he is to register the feelings of others. He eats hardly anything, sitting erect and leaning slightly forward, his hands in his lap, as he makes extended speeches at Betsy. She, in turn, does only a slightly better job at perceiving him. She invents him, or romanticizes him, when she applies the words of a Kris Kristofferson song to him ("he's a poet and a pusher, partly truth and partly fiction, a walking contradiction"). The gulf that separates them is too great, though for him it doesn't exist at all.

Travis doesn't understand that you don't take nice girls like Betsy to porno movies, particularly on the first date. For him, such movies are standard fare after a night's work behind the wheel and he can't sleep. In one sequence he sits with his fingers in front of his eyes, partially obscuring his vision. He both wants to look and not to look at the screen. Earlier, he naïvely attempts to introduce himself to the young woman behind the candy counter at a porno theater. Her rebuff prefigures Betsy's rejection. For him, Betsy is now "just like the others, cold and distant." He bursts into the campaign headquarters and tells Betsy she's in hell and he is then ejected. Schrader, at this point, provides a telling sequence which underlines Travis' growing sickness. Scorsese himself plays a distressed man who asks Travis to stop the cab outside an apartment in which his wife is having a rendezvous with a black man. She is clearly visible in the window as Scorsese tells Travis at length what damage he's going to do with a .44 Magnum to her face and her "pussy." The scene is full of sexual laceration. In its fantasy of violent sexual revenge, Scorsese plays the role of a substitute figure for Travis. He's an extension of Travis' rage, but a more articulate and uncensored one. That his wife has a black lover is not accidental. From the fancy-dressed pimps in the coffee shop to the kids hassling the whores in the street nearby to the robber in the market, blacks are a focus of Travis' anger and paranoia.

Another failure of communication occurs when Travis tries to confide in Wizzard. He wants to tell him about his growing sickness, but he can't articulate it. There's real poignance in his stifled cry for help. "I got some bad ideas in my head. I just want to go out and really do something." There's more than a failure of language—more than caution—going on here. The feelings he has are too deep, too tormenting to put into words. Wizzard takes his complaints to be job related and starts waxing philosophical ("there's no choice; we're all fucked up") and tells Travis to "get laid." This is the only time in the film when Travis tries to open up his deepest self to another person, and it is a total failure. Of course, that self is beyond him or beside him—out of reach. No wonder he can't describe it.

Just before the assassination attempt, Travis confides in his diary: "Now I see it clearly; my whole life has pointed in one direction. I see that now. There never has been any choice for me." This statement of fatedness contains no rational program; he hasn't come to any thoughtful conclusions about his choices. It's a giving way to the surge of despair within. De Niro's intonation as he speaks the lines is full of sadness and resignation. The killing of the black man in the market may have something to do with this. It's an interesting scene in its own right, filmed in a very natural, documentary-like style and is a good example of Scorsese's realism in *Taxi Driver*. In its seventeen shots there's no attempt to overdramatize the incident. It's recorded like a commonplace, daily event. The setting is a real *tienda* or small Latino store with old-style white tile floor, a glass-fronted cold box, and a few aisles of goods. Travis is greeted as a regular customer by the owner and their exchanges throughout are matter-of-fact. In shot 2 Travis enters with slow, tense, tired steps and proceeds to the back where he makes a selection and hears the robber threatening the owner; he pauses momentarily, thinking what to do while the camera circles to show him slowly approaching the robber from the rear, still holding his clipboard under his arm, his purchase in one hand, and his gun in the other. The fast shots which follow show the shooting and its aftermath though Scorsese keeps the camera at a distance, using overhead angles and medium shots. "Did you get him?" asks the owner; "I got him," Travis replies. "Is he dead?" "I don't know; his eyes are moving," says Travis as he puts his foot on the hand holding the gun. In shots 6 and 7 the owner comes around the cold box and probes the robber with a metal bar which he then uses to beat the corpse-like man whom he has propped up against the box as Travis leaves. The visual procedure here is very different from the final sequence of carnage which ends the film, with its wild, lurid, expressionistic effects. The matter-of-factness here exactly suits Travis' state of mind. He hasn't gone overboard yet. The documentary style functions nicely here as a ground against which the increasingly distorted images of Travis' despair can be measured. In the next scene, he's holding the .44 Magnum he's bought as he gazes depressed and unblinking at young couples dancing on TV. The camera, like Travis' mind, moves slowly, absorbedly toward the TV screen until it fills the frame. The young dancers move to the music as the camera continues to push into their space, noticing a pair of shoes on the floor. It's a surreal image, but of what? Absence, loneliness? The sequence is a repetition of the Alka-Seltzer shots. At any rate, the shooting in the market seems to have brought him closer to the acts of attempted and actual violence with which the film culminates.

The relationship between Travis and the young prostitute, Iris (Jodie Foster), is carefully prepared. He first encounters her when she's trying to get away from Sport, who drags her out of the cab and throws a crumpled twenty dollar bill at Travis and tells him to forget about this incident. Travis immediately perceives her as a victim of the street vermin he abhors. He keeps the crumpled twenty when, on several occasions, he has the chance to spend it. It's dirty money, but it also functions like a talisman associated with Iris. He only gives it up when he tips the man who rents the room where Iris takes her customers, returning it to its corrupt source. Earlier, when he happens to see Iris hook up with a customer, he abruptly pulls away from the curb. There's a suggestion of sexual attraction here, but it isn't present at all when he finally goes to her room. This scene is one of the most revealing in the film and is worth looking at closely. Before doing so, however, I want to look briefly at the scene with Sport, which leads into it.

Travis' tension-filled body language, which I've mentioned earlier, intensifies as Sport goes into an animated and lurid description of what Travis can do with the twelve-and-a-half-year-old girl (she is probably a year or two older). De Niro's posture subtly but clearly suggests his growing rage at Sport. Travis is facing half away from Sport, wearing dark glasses. He has a fixed, mask-like smile, which dissolves into an angry frown as he turns away and moves toward Iris. He turns to look back at Sport several times as he and Iris walk along. The signals here, and they are almost entirely nonverbal, suggest that his rage at Sport is the determining factor at this moment in his relationship with Iris—that he's only interested in her as Sport's victim. It doesn't seem far-fetched to imagine that he makes his decision to kill Sport during this encounter.

The scene in Iris' room is important because it dramatizes a break-down in Travis' isolation and his first real connection with another person. In some ways, it's like the scenes between Raskolnikov and the "holy" prostitute Sonia in *Crime and Punishment*. The Dostoyevsky novel as well as *Notes from the Underground* lies like a hidden text beneath Schrader's personal utterance. The scene in the movie is four minutes and forty seconds long and is made up of forty-nine shots—or about one shot every six seconds—and yet the cutting has fluidity and naturalness which flow out of the dialogue, the cuts being largely determined by who is speaking at the moment.

After Travis' tense, suspicion-dominated entry (Iris has to turn back and call out "Come on," almost as if she were speaking to a child), the first thing we're apt to notice is the strange decor. This isn't the plain, anonymous room where quick sex takes place, but a neat, somewhat hippie-like pad. There are about thirty or forty candles burning on two tables in the corner and on the mantelpiece. It's like a shrine or a sanctuary—especially so for Travis, who will experience a momentary sense of healing in its confines. We're asked to overlook the obvious fire danger from the candles while Sport and Iris are out in the street. There are posters of popular entertainers on one wall, and a mandala-like picture on another. A fringed shade emits soft light from a bulb hanging from the ceiling. This is obviously someone's bedroom, perhaps Iris' and Sport's, though the rather narrow bed suggests otherwise. (A later scene in which Sport bends Iris' mind to his devices, while they are dancing together, shows that it is their bedroom—when Sport happens to be around.)

Travis immediately questions Iris about her age and, because of his persistence, learns her real name, which she says she detests (she's probably in flight from her family). He's not at all interested in sex with her; his demonstrations of this grow more assertive as she persists in trying to arouse him. His violence is, in part, an acting out of sexual repression. His appetite for porno movies seems based in sexual disgust rather than arousal. He's not fully present in his body; his mental obsessions continue to drive him. When she tells him she doesn't remember entering his cab to get away from Sport, he dismisses her with "Well, that's all right. I'm going to get you out of here." She denies a sense of connection to him, but his plan is impervious to her feelings. At this point she exists for him only as Sport's innocent victim. Her excuse that she must have been stoned when she got in the cab provokes him to respond, "They drugged you?" Her response to him to "Come off it" says that he's more innocent than she is. And yet there's a sense in which she's innocent or unhardened, too, for at the end of the scene she's touched by Travis' concern for her and cares about his feelings.

At the midpoint, however, she's careful like Betsy in responding to his aggressiveness (he has already pushed her down on the couch and then, a moment later, thrown her on the couch after she kneels down and quickly unzips his pants). She hesitantly repeats his words about his reasons for rescuing her; she doesn't want things to get out of hand. She tells him she got into his cab because "I was stoned," and that "When I'm stoned I got no place else to go." Presumably referring to Sport and the other handlers in the prostitution ring, she says, "They just protect me from myself." This muddled reasoning disarms Travis. Shaking his head slowly, he rises to leave, saying, "I don't know. . . . Well, I tried." At this point, in shot 45, Iris reaches out to touch him and tells him his concern for her really means something. He asks her if he can see her again, but his eyes are closed as he speaks; he still hasn't emerged from his self-enclosure. After he tells her his name, he reaches out open-eyed and touches her face, saying,

"Sweet Iris." The connection between then now is as much real as imagined. It's real in the sense that Travis has actually perceived a quality of innocence in Iris and responded to it. It's also imaginary in that her innocence merely happens to accord with his needed fantasy of female purity ("They cannot touch her"), which is the other side of his view of women as debased, filthy, sexual objects (the porno films, the whores in the streets). Nevertheless, the momentary personal connection in this scene suggests that Travis' interest in Iris may possibly develop beyond his hatred for Sport. Some change has occurred within him. She remains touched and perplexed, her arms across her chest as he leaves.

The scene in Iris' room is bracketed by dark and threatening images of the narrow, dimly lit halls of the building and the man who collects the rent. In the five-shot sequence after Travis leaves, the atmosphere is particularly unsettling. The softening we've seen in him with Iris evaporates as soon as he closes the door. The warm, lyrical sax melody fades as his face tenses and darkens and the threatening theme of chorded horns returns (these two themes are utilized by Bernard Herrmann from the opening sequence of the film to the end). The man emerges out of the darkness of the far end of the hall, his right hand raised to receive a tip, and Travis gives him the crumpled twenty dollars saying, "This is yours" (this belongs to you). The brief sequence is filled with menace. When Travis tells the man he'll return, he may have already decided to return shooting.

In the breakfast scene the next day with Iris, he pursues his angry feelings about Sport, just as he'd been angry about Tom to Betsy. Nevertheless, there's an easiness of communication between them that contrasts with the coffee shop scene with Betsy. Despite their differences in age, they're on the same wavelength: they're both people from rather strict backgrounds who have dropped out. Iris talks about astrology and communes in Vermont. She's like one of those flower children who went to Haight-Ashbury in San Francisco in the '70s, after the bloom had degenerated into hard drugs and prostitution. She even asks Travis if he'd like to go with her to Vermont. She thinks she can just split, but he knows that it will be harder for her to get out. He's relaxed, and smiles a lot. He promises to give her money to help her and says he may be away for a while. The friendship promised in the scene in her room seems to be growing.

The scene in which Travis guns down Sport and the others is, in many respects, the culmination of *Taxi Driver*. It is also one of the most horrifying and painful scenes of violence in an American cinema soaked in violence. Scorsese doesn't make the violence operatic or romantic (as in the *Godfather* films), or sanctioned by a good cause (patriotism or the justified revenge as in the *Rambo* films). It is like the violence in Visconti's *Rocco and His Brothers*—straight, unadorned, brutal. Perhaps for these reasons, a repeated viewing of the scene is difficult for the viewer; his senses never go numb as they do more easily with scenes in which violence is presented as a form of entertainment (with the appropriate music, exaggerated sound effects, and bravura camera work).

The scene is composed of fifty-seven shots, many of them very fast and jarring. Having armed himself with three guns and a knife, Travis first shoots Sport in the stomach. Then, after sitting on the steps for a while, he goes into the narrow hallway and wounds the man who collects the room money from Iris' customers. A mafia collection man rushes out of Iris' room, and Travis shoots him next. Unlike scenes of romanticized or sanitized violence, no one dies quickly. Sport reappears and wounds Travis in the neck before he is finally felled by a blast from the huge .44 magnum. Parenthetically, the film is careful in its detailing of the varying degrees of bodily damage which can be done by guns of differing caliber. The gun obsession of Americans is most accurately presented in the matter-of-fact sequence in which Travis purchases his weapons from Handy Andy, who lays out his varied assortment and gives a detailed description of each. Andy is played by Stephen Prince who was raised by a gun-loving father and who is the subject of the short *American Boy*. To return to the sequence, the room rent collector has most of his right hand blown off (the same hand that received the crumpled twenty dollars) as he emerges from the dark recesses of the hall. Travis shoots him in the body with the .38 pistol and clubs him as he heads upstairs for Iris' room, but the collector keeps coming after him, shouting over and over again, "I'll kill you, I'll kill you." He grabs Travis outside Iris' door as the mafioso emerges and shoots Travis from one foot away. Falling to the floor, Travis activates the pistol he's rigged up on a metal slide along his arm. The gun pops into his hand and he fires about eight shots into the mafioso, who staggers back through the beaded curtain and falls dead at Iris' feet. He finally finishes the rent collector by shooting him in the head after stabbing him through the hand as they struggle on the floor next to the dead mafioso. Travis then puts the gun to his own head and fires four times, but it is out of ammunition, as is the gun on the slide which he fires at the couch next to where Iris is collapsed in horror.

The final shot of the sequence is, in many ways, the most telling. As the police enter, their guns drawn, Travis leans back on the couch where his is sitting, a half-smile on his face, and points the index finger of his blood-soaked hand at his temple. He "fires" three times, making a sound effect with his mouth each time. The scene lasts nearly six minutes (5:55 to be exact) and is cinematically interesting in several respects, particularly in its handling of visual space. In shots 5–9 there's a fine, fast "echo" sequence as the sound from Travis' first shot at the rent collector goes up the stairs and into Iris' room, startling her. It's not an accurate shot in terms of the actual speed of sound, of course, but it shows how Iris becomes alerted in graphic visual terms. It also shows in advance the path the violence will take as it moves up the stairs into Iris' room. Iris' alarm is shown in a fast shot as she turns her head quickly to see where the sound is coming from, but Scorsese uses slow motion to the shot. Slow motion is also used when Travis goes up the stairs and when the mafioso comes out of the room with his gun drawn. In these shots the slow motion is modified (about two-thirds actual speed) so that it doesn't call attention to itself, unlike the slow-motion scenes of carnage at the end of *Bonnie and Clyde*, for example. For the most part, the scene has the same natural, functional rhythm in its images as the shooting in the market. It's like a well-made documentary. There are two exceptions, however. The shot in which the rent collector's hand is blown half away is close to the excesses of Peckinpahean violence, and the shots (numbers 44 and 45) in which Travis stabs the collector's hand fall completely into that domain. They are a gratuitous keying-up of the already overwhelming violence in order to titillate the audience. Travis' own quiet demonstration of his desire to kill himself (the finger to the temple) is much more powerful. He's fully in the grip of the death urge by this time. He's gone beyond his hatred for Sport and the other street vermin. If he had the bullets, he'd kill anyone—except Iris.

The aftermath, or winding down, of the violence is introduced by a fine overhead shot of the policemen with their guns drawn. Scorsese pivots his camera in this position, giving the shot a particularly effective twisting motion and then the camera moves slowly out of the room and down the stairs. The slow movement here is particularly appropriate to a denouement after convulsive violence. The slow rhythm of the shots and the heavy brass chords of Herrmann's score serve to accentuate the frantic violence of the prior sequence. The walls of the graffiti-covered halls are spattered with blood; Sport's body lies near the street door. These images have an almost hallucinatory, dreamlike distortion. Slow motion is used once again as police cars and medical personnel assemble in front of the apartment building.

The remainder of *Taxi Driver* involves a kind of epilogue that, at least for this writer, tends to diminish the film. We see Travis, recuperated from his wounds, visiting with his fellow cab drivers. The three prior meetings with the drivers have functioned to illustrate his growing alienation. Now he looks better, more relaxed and fully present. Clippings on the wall of his room tell us he's been portrayed in the press as a hero for rescuing Iris. We hear her father's voice reading a letter to Travis and, despite its hopefulness and thankfulness, there's an ominous note hidden there: we'll never give Iris cause to leave our safety again. She's trapped in the same environment she fled. Betsy gets into Travis' cab, in what probably is no accident, but he refuses her interest in him. He seems calm inside, no longer obsessed with her, as he leaves her at the curb. Some viewers have taken this segment of the film to be a fantasy on Travis' part. It is clear, however, that he's less removed from reality than before.

Travis seems really to have changed inside. You'd think a man so deeply traumatized would be even more haunted and edgy. It's as if the explosion of violence has washed him clean and left him at peace. This can't be called a religious transformation, and yet it approaches that condition. As he lacks political ideology, so he lacks religious conviction. His violence can't be said to have brought spiritual awakening. There is no evidence that Travis has experienced any guilt in the manner of Raskolnikov in *Crime and Punishment*, or that guilt brought him spiritual rebirth. Scorsese is careful not to push the idea of spiritual change through violence, so common in his later films, in Travis' case. Yet he seems softer, more open. The irony of his heroism looks forward to Rupert Pupkin's celebrity status at the end of *The King of Comedy*. Still, the ending serves to soften the violence (a commercial necessity?) and suggests even the promise of romance for Travis. Betsy's face floats in his rearview mirror, her hair is wind-blown, her expression warm and interested. Only in the final three shots do we see Travis glancing anxiously and nervously as he looks around for another fare. These shots could have been taken from the opening of the film and were most likely shot at the same time as those in the opening. They and the images behind the final credits as well as the music suggest that nothing has really changed.

The historical immediacy of *Taxi Driver* was demonstrated by John Hinckley's assassination attempt on President Reagan. As details of the crime emerged, it became clear that Hinckley took the film as his operative text, pursuing Jodie Foster both before the attempt (at Yale in person) and afterward (by mail). His identification with Travis demonstrated that

Schrader and Scorsese had put their fingers on at least one dimension of the profile of one kind of political assassin (lonely, antisocial, obsessive-compulsive, lacking political ideology). There is one unmistakable reference to a historical assassination in the film. When Travis buys his pistols from the illegal gun dealer, he points one of them down from the hotel room at a throughway, tracking a moving car. The reference is to Oswald's shots from the Texas School Book Depository down to the moving vehicle in which John Kennedy was riding.

Notes

1. Paul Schrader, *Taxi Driver* (London: Faber and Faber, 1990), 16.
2. Scorsese has remarked that this shot was "the first shot I thought of in the film and the last I filmed." *Scorsese on Scorsese*, 54.

Chapter 5

A NEW, NEW MUSICAL

NEW YORK, NEW YORK, 1977;
THE LAST WALTZ, 1978;
AMERICAN BOY, 1978

New York, New York

New York, New York appeared in 1977. *Taxi Driver*'s unexpected success a year earlier led to a certain euphoria on Scorsese's part, which caused problems in *New York, New York*. Hearing that Irwin Winkler wanted to produce a film on the Big Band Era, he went after the project with relish. He'd grown up with Hollywood musicals by Minnelli, Cukor, and others, and he wanted to make a musical film that was both a tribute to these films and a serious examination of the musical life. With potent young stars like Liza Minnelli and De Niro and with a fine cluster of songs by John Kander and Fred Ebb, and with plenty of money, everything seemed promising. True, the film turned out to be too long at 163 minutes, but it remains a fine, interesting, only somewhat flawed film. Its failure seems to have occurred with a public that didn't like Scorsese tampering with a tried-and-true genre: the happy musical. The simplistic, almost prepackaged tastes of the American moviegoer caused the failure, not anything inherently poor in the film.

New York, New York may be too long, but it is rich with invention and real-life complexity. It is a study of the conflicted relationship between two creative musicians, both a tribute to and a parody of '40s musicals, a realistic presentation of the road life of a big band, and a study of the typical Scorsese hero: an obsessive/compulsive sax musician played by De Niro. Most of all, it is a fine film about music.

The long opening sequence in which Jimmy Doyle (De Niro) meets Francine Evans (Minnelli) establishes the conflicted relationship very well. It's the night celebrating the end of World War II (V.J.-Day), and a crowd is dancing to the music of the Glenn Miller Band. Jimmy, in a florid short-sleeved shirt, is circulating briskly, looking for an attractive woman. He keeps coming back to Francine who's in her army uniform, though she repeatedly rejects him. He's persistently obnoxious, with a cocky, wise-guy look on his face. The signal from him is clear: if you want any kind of relationship with me, it's going to be one with conflict built in. Francine never vigorously tells him to get lost: she's a nice, somewhat passive young woman of her time—thirty years or so before the widespread women's movement of the '70s and '80s. She, in effect, allows Jimmy to impose himself on her. When we learn, somewhat to our surprise, that she's an accomplished musician in her own right, we're probably puzzled by her acceptance of his persistent aggressive attentions. She can stand on her own. Why does she need him? More than the period music of Glenn Miller and the Big Band Era, Francine's behavior is of its time. She's a nice girl, without being uptight. She's also another of Scorsese's depic-tions of the unthreatening woman. Jimmy, on the other hand, is not a nice boy. As De Niro articulates him, he's both witty and inventive, and strange, a kind of musical Rupert Pupkin in *The King of Comedy*. He can't stop; he can't take "no" for an answer. He's an extremist. He likes chaos and angry emotional displays; she likes order and a certain amount of calmness. In this sense they are complementary. Their differences in character are expressed in their music. Francine sings the conventional ballads and show-biz melodies; Jimmy likes it best when he's hanging out with black musicians playing hard-edged, improvisational solos. He's on the "cutting edge." The conflict between them is a musical conflict as well as a career and personality conflict. The fact that Francine constantly rescues Jimmy's role with the band is a problem for him. It gives him power but also confines him to the kind of music he resents having to perform.

The opening scene of the V.J.-Day celebration is indicative of the strengths and weaknesses of the film. The sequences have an interesting look—a highly artificial, studio-arranged background like the old musicals with a contrasting realism of foreground action in which Jimmy pursues Francine in the midst of the celebration, which also seems staged as if it's part of the background. It's as if Scorsese is saying "this film isn't going to conform entirely to the old conventions; it's going to play with them and also do something new." But his decision to let De Niro and Minnelli improvise the first encounter between their characters means that the sequence is full of excellent, spontaneous acting, and also that it goes on for twenty minutes. Unlike his earlier efforts. Scorsese had not story-boarded a tight script for *New York, New York.* He gave the actors their heads and then couldn't rein them in. A careful scrutiny of this episode, with an eye to removing footage, reveals the problem confronting Scorsese. Each encounter between Jimmy and Francine in the dancing crowd flows seamlessly into the next; nothing can come out or the whole is ruined. Scorsese wants to show her gradual submission to his advances but it's too gradual. The sequence is interesting, but it lacks tight structure. The length of the sequence is also determined by Scorsese's desire to pay tribute to the music. Thus we have the Miller rendition of "Ciri Biri Bin" in its entirety, as well as other Big Band numbers. A tighter, more elliptical presentation of the V.J.-Day celebration might have benefitted the whole film, but it would have cheated the music—and this is true for some other musical sequences. The original cut of the V.J.-Day sequence ran one hour and took four weeks to shoot. Another reason, besides the music, that it is so long has to do with improvisation:

> We were trying to keep the technique of improvisation and documentary approach in the foreground, with the artifice of the fake sets in the background. But you have to build the sets in advance, which means you're not being practical, because once you start improvising in one set you soon improvise your way out of that set into another situation. In the mean-

> time, they're building a different set because it's in the script!
> So you have to go back and shoot some more to get yourself
> back in line to use that second set—and that's one of the
> reasons why the scenes are so long.[1]

This problem in the opening sequence was true for the whole film which ran 270 minutes (4 ½ hours) in its initial cut, and had to be pared down to nearly half the length for release.

The problems inherent in Scorsese's use of improvisation are best seen in *New York, New York*. When used judiciously and within a careful structure, improvisation adds authenticity and documentary realism, as in the scene in *Raging Bull* when Jake asks Joey, "Did you fuck my wife?" for example. When improvisation is allowed to defeat any controls, the result can be disastrous. Scorsese's retrospective appraisal is judicious: "I don't think we should have been given that free a hand. It was a mess, and it's a miracle the film makes any kind of sense."[2] What saved the film, of course, was brilliant editing. Films with tight budgets have a better chance of artistic success.

Nonmusical sequences are also inflated: the violent argument between Jimmy and Francine in the moving car, the whispered separation in the hospital, the scene on the doorstep of the home of the Justice of the Peace, the discussion about whether Francine should return to New York to have the baby. The acting in all these sequences is fine but they are too long. The sequence in which Jimmy observes a sailor and his girl dancing in a spotlight from a stairway near the elevated subway is very nice but it could come out without damage to the whole. The virtues of directorial control are amply demonstrated in two musical sequences which were carefully structured before shooting: the "Honeysuckle Rose" scene in the black nightclub and the "Happy Endings" musical theater sequence toward the end of the film. The "Happy Endings" sequence was removed a few weeks before the film opened in order to shorten it. One of the film's best sequences was chopped because others couldn't be pared down.

The reason the "Honeysuckle Rose" sequence is so tight and structured is not hard to find. There are a number of things going on in it and Scorsese has to keep track of them all in an economical fashion. It's not like the two-character give-and-take exchanges between Francine and Jimmy that run on. Jimmy and Francine, several months pregnant, have entered the black nightclub where Jimmy is playing in order to discuss a big recording contract Decca Records is offering Francine. This discussion occurs at a table at the far end of the room above the dance floor and the bandstand. Jimmy's edginess in the face of Francine's success renders him nearly mute. He leaves to make a phone call and, in one of the key shots, we see him complete his call while looking at the women going upstairs, and then he stands contemplatively for a good fifteen seconds as he broods upon Francine's success. A gorgeous black singer (Diahnne Abbott) comes down the stairs and gives Jimmy a light verbal jab about family night as she brushes off his attempt to touch her. The camera stays on Jimmy as the singer begins "Honeysuckle Rose," then moves over to pick up the band and singer, swinging off musical phrases from the sax and horn to pick up the singer's answering responses. It's fresh and vital work on the actors' and Scorsese's part and helps us understand why Jimmy loves this life. The sequence also brings the music alive cinematically without giving us the whole song.

Francine is now alone at the table, getting drunk while Jimmy joins the band. She approaches through the audience and stands looking up appreciatively at Jimmy while he solos, but when she gets up on the stage Jimmy turns the solo into a harsh, angry series of utterances. He can't stand her success and tells her through his sax to get away from what little turf he has left. He construes her success as diminishing him. He's not really a secure man. He can't celebrate his wife's success and feel good for her. Instead, he becomes angry and subversive, increasing his attentions to other women. He may be a gifted artist—more gifted than she—but he's an incomplete man. Jimmy's distress is all done in a musical setting and through the music—another example of Scorsese's interesting revisionist tribute to '40s musicals. His anger and anguish are best heard in the high harsh vibrato phrases the sax emits as he glares at her. Surprisingly, the band picks up Jimmy's radical change of tempo and phrasing with enthusiasm; he's a hot performer. The players might just as easily have shown some confusion at what Jimmy is doing. In this, and numerous other occasions, he's revealed as a creative player who can't or won't play in ensemble fashion. He's better in small improvisational groups than in tightly arranged big bands, but even there his aggressive style tends to take over. He refuses to play in the style of the traveling big band, "taking off" on his own constantly. He bullies and demeans the other players in the band when he becomes the temporary leader. The leader of the band, nicely played by Georgie Auld who does the sax solos in the film, puts it pungently to Francine as they travel on the bus: Jimmy can blow a lot of sax "but he's a top pain in the ass." Francine constantly bails him out by smoothing the feelings he has hurt. The scene which depicts this looks like another improvisation between Minnelli and De Niro and takes up too much space, yet it is very evocative. After soothing the band's feelings,

she gives the downbeat to start over again and Jimmy explodes, humiliating her in front of the band ("Don't ever do that again, you hear me?").
She rehearses her song in tears.

She rescues him in an early tryout for a job by stepping forward and
singing to his sax (this is the first time we learn she's a singer). The lyrics
she sings say:

> I'll work and slave the whole day through,
> So I can hurry home to you,
> 'Cause you brought a new kind of love to me.

She appears to need his seemingly dominant aggressiveness, his put
downs. Underneath, however, he is dependent on her nurturing, loving
spirit; he needs her to make things right and he hates his dependency on
her and her success.

In the hospital scene, an interesting breakup scene underplayed almost
entirely in whispers, Jimmy tells her he can't handle the new baby and that
he needs her comfort (though he stayed away from her during much of her
pregnancy). His dependency is as great a source of anger toward her as
their career conflicts.

The "Happy Endings" sequence, which was removed at the last
moment prior to the film's release, is deservedly celebrated by film buffs.
It has the same structured quality as the sequence in the black jazz club
though it deals with a different kind of music—Francine's style of musical
theater. It's a witty celebration and affectionate parody of the dance
musicals of the '40s, particularly the films of Vincente Minnelli.
Francine's discovery by a handsome producer, who has lost his glove in
the theater, leads to several song and dance sequences (shot in parody of
the conventional musicals) in which she has become a star. The producer
rejects her love because he wouldn't want to be known as the appendage
to a famous performer, and she wakes up as an usherette only to have the
fantasy begin all over again, replete with images of the star in a feathered
boa descending a vast glittering staircase à la Rita Hayworth. Suddenly we
see that Jimmy has been watching "Happy Endings" in a packed,
enthusiastic theater. This film within a film presents Francine's fame, her
lover's fear of her fame, and her loneliness all wrapped in the romantic
confection of the "A Star Is Born" musical. It's a charming and effective
piece of movie making. Its subtlety allows it to be enjoyed simply for what
it is, or, for those with a sense of movie history, for its playful references
to earlier popular films and stage productions. Its removal seems almost
perverse, but was, again, the result of the bloated earlier footage.

Francine's fame is complemented by Jimmy's own. He has his own club, and it is lavish, with his own cool group and a revolving stage for another black group which plays feverishly and experimentally. He's less edgy, more self-contained, stronger, and definitely successful financially. We don't know how he managed to get this way—the major subject matter of Scorsese's films. There's a buried story here: how Jimmy moves from reckless, ultimately self-punishing behavior (à la Jake LaMotta, or even Travis Bickle) to a saner, more successful life. That story would be saved for the next film. Somehow Jimmy's good fortune is less convincing than that of Francine. He looks like a brilliant loser through much of the film. We could easily imagine him strung out, blowing intense ragged solos in a less prosperous setting. Perhaps it's well to remember that a great sax player like Stan Getz managed a successful career despite horrible heroin addiction and insanely abusive behavior. Somehow Jimmy has managed to make it without Francine. He doesn't need her any more, nor she him. That is why they don't get together for a late dinner after one of her nightclub performances which he has witnessed. His feelings aren't really hurt as he walks away from the softly lit, empty, rain-soaked street where they were to have met. It's the last poignant shot in the film and perfectly evokes a relationship that wasn't meant to last. Evidently the audience wanted its fantasies totally satisfied—they wanted a real "Happy Ending," not a pretend or parodied one, or a poignant, unhappy one. The ending to the film is precisely right for a film which mixes romantic film conventions with a realistic treatment of human behavior. It's also, unlike what has gone before, a concise, economical, and quiet ending. In years to come, the film may come to be regarded as one of the most inventive American musical films.

The commercial failure of *New York, New York* was a deep blow to Scorsese, causing protracted emotional distress. He felt he had finally made a film that would please the film public at large, in the Hollywood style, and his disappointment ran deep. The euphoric self-indulgence in which the film was made gave way to depression and continued self-indulgence in the way of drugs. The crisis which followed saw Scorsese in the hospital and ultimately contributed to the making of *Raging Bull.*

The Last Waltz

Scorsese's one feature-length documentary, *The Last Waltz* (1978), is a record of the last concert given by The Band in San Francisco in November 1976. It's another treatment of music, like *New York, New York*, but in a different mode. Lead by Robbie Robertson, The Band was one of the leading rock groups of the '60s. Scorsese was finishing final shooting on *New York, New York* and faced with the daunting task of editing the ungainly footage into some kind of coherent form when he was contacted by Jonathan Taplin about the documentary. Perhaps it's a sign of Scorsese's nearly out-of-control life at this point that he accepted the project. His own self-admitted cocaine-filled energy probably induced him to immerse himself in the rock environment. *The Last Waltz* is commonly regarded as the best rock and roll documentary and has been revived to popular acclaim in 2002.

The Band was a group of accomplished Canadian musicians with one American, the galvanic singer-drummer Levon Helm. One purpose of the documentary was to record the group's variety (from country and folk to bluegrass and rock) as well as the varied skills of each member, most of whom could play three or four instruments. The group had achieved early success as Bob Dylan's backup band, so Dylan is there to contribute to their send-off as well as Neil Young, Joni Mitchell, Paul Butterfield, and Van Morrison, among others. The Band's numbers are mixed with high-energy performances by these luminaries, which provide further variety and drive. Scorsese's interviews with the members of The Band are probably the weakest part of the film. He's on record as saying that he's a lousy interviewer. Still, the film has a high quality despite most of the interviews and a few performances by The Band's guests. This is all the more remarkable considering that Scorsese had virtually no lead time between agreeing to the project and the concert itself—about six weeks. In a spasm of frantic energy he produced a shooting script of 200 pages and planned the placement for seven cameras to shoot in 35 mm and full synchronized sound.

The Last Waltz is more than a documentary of a memorable concert. It's a film about music, shot and edited in a musical way. It's no accident that the superb jazz sequences in *New York, New York* (particularly the nightclub sequence in which Diahnne Abbott sings "Honeysuckle Rose") and the concert sequences in the documentary were edited at about the same time. The two films are the high points of Scorsese's cinematic treatment of music and a great deal of credit must go to his and Thelma

Schoonmaker's conscientious piecing together of the raw footage. *The Last Waltz* wasn't released for two years, because the editing of both films took so much time and *New York, New York* needed to be finished first.

The musicality of the film is first seen in Neil Young's performance of "Helpless." The cutting serves to accentuate not only the rhythm of the song but also Young's desire to extend the singing to members of The Band and ultimately to the audience. We see shots of Young glancing smilingly at Robertson and Rick Danko, the lead singer, as he enlists their participation in the chorus, and shots as well of Joni Mitchell backlit backstage as she responds, "I can hear you now." The effect is one of group enterprise, of communal celebration—the pure spirit of the '60s at its best. Oddly, there are no shots of its audience as it responds to Young's "Sing with me now." Scorsese's decision to omit the audience and keep the focus on stage throughout the film, a crucial and excellent decision, seems a limiting factor here—but only here. *The Last Waltz* is a film without reaction shots. Neil Diamond's inclusion in the filmed concert is a stark contrast. Standing isolated in the cone of light, Diamond delivers a synthetic star-turn totally out of keeping with the rest of the performances.

The Band's skill as arrangers as well as musicians is seen in "Nazareth" and "The Night They Drove Old Dixie Down," two of their hits. In the first number the use of a chorus of four African-American singers adds excitement as does the brass chorus in "Dixie." In both numbers the camera begins by moving in on Levon Helm as he voices the lyrics. In "Nazareth" there's a cut to a shot behind the lead choral singer which pivots to reveal her three companions as they join her in song. This shot and others like it in "Nazareth" is undoubtedly one Scorsese planned in his shooting script, perhaps based on rehearsal. Like the musical sequences in *New York, New York* it's an example of his skills in a controlled environment. The Band's concert was hardly a controlled environment. "I hardly got any of my planned moves, because once The Band started playing you couldn't hear a thing."[3] It's amazing that any musical choreography is achieved. In fact, throughout the film the cutting and camera movement serve to heighten the music.

Two other performances deserve attention. In "Coyote" Joni Mitchell delivers by far the most interesting lyrics in the form of a narrative poem. Because her words are so important and because she stays close to a fixed mike Scorsese wisely gives us long takes in medium close-up and hardly directs our attention to the other performers. In contrast Van Morrison's dancing improvisations on a single refrain are full of electric energy and the fast cutting and mobile framing pick up his interactions with the members of The Band.

The decision to add studio-shot sequences by Emmy Lou Harris (standing far apart from The Band with artificial fog rolling in) and a final number by The Band is an unfortunate one, evidently occasioned by Universal Studios' late contribution of money and Robbie Robertson's continual suggestions for modification during the two-year period between shooting and release. The film should rightly end with Bob Dylan's and all the other performers' last number "I Shall Be Released" as the camera pulls back to a long shot of the stage. Instead we have a brief interview between Scorsese and Robertson about the hard life on the road, then a bridge passage to an odd number in which Levon Helm plays a mandolin. The versatility of The Band is demonstrated but the music and setting are totally out of character with what has gone before. The attempt to bring us back inside Winterland Arena where the film was shot by using sounds of the departing musicians and crowd behind the credits doesn't work.

One small shot in the film seems especially significant. At the very end of "Dixie," as the music rises to a keen pitch, there's a cut to Robertson rising into the frame. It's a good shot, complementing the thrust of the music. The only odd thing about it is that Robertson has largely been a passive accompanist; the number has been driven by Helm as lead singer. The shot was of course chosen by Scorsese and indicates his interest in Robertson. As a leader Robertson sets the tempo and indicates entrances and exits but in terms of musical voicing he remains a background figure. He has four small guitar solos in the whole film and never sings by himself. He's the farthest thing from the great rock singer and guitarist John Fogerty of Creedence Clearwater Revival. Yet the camera notices him more than the others. He stands slightly forward, a long scarf casually draped over his neck. He's the least animated of his group and yet seems to compel the most attention. He's Mr. Cool, the unmoved mover, a companion spirit to Warhol. In the interviews he is most often the central speaker, making gnomic utterances ("It's the end of the beginning of the ending"). Scorsese seems mesmerized by him. He's a fine example of the importance of so-called personality and celebrity in rock, in which the music almost seems secondary. The best example is, of course, Mick Jagger. In this sense *The Last Waltz* seems about all of rock and roll, not just the music.

Scorsese's subsequent involvement with Robertson in hard drugs and nonstop movie watching while they were roommates in the Hollywood

Hills ultimately lead to a physical breakdown and the making of *Raging Bull.*

American Boy

American Boy, Scorsese's fifty-five minute film, is rarely seen. Never released commercially or in video or DVD, there are apparently only half a dozen or less prints in existence. In effect it's only available to the general public at Scorsese retrospectives. It was shot in 1978, the same year as *The Last Waltz*, and two years before *Raging Bull*. The reasons for its obscurity are probably threefold: its length, its documentary nature, and its haphazard structure which only builds to real interest at the very end.

The film is, in effect, a series of stories told by Scorsese's friend Stephen Prince intercut with home movie footage from Prince's infancy. The subject is drugs and guns, though Prince regales his audience of Scorsese and friends with other tales of a pet gorilla, a drunken sailing experience, how he made money as a boy selling bagels, how he avoided the draft by telling the examiners he'd had a homosexual experience. In his mid- to late twenties at the time of the film, he's an accomplished raconteur, the kind of performer whom Scorsese would logically cast in the role of Handy Andy who provides Travis Bickle with his armory of guns in *Taxi Driver*. *American Boy* has been coupled with *Taxi Driver* though it seems in many ways more connected to *The Last Waltz* both in its documentary structure and its autobiographical subtext: Scorsese's own heavy use of drugs in this period. Prince is a less charismatic version of Robbie Robertson. Scorsese is not behind the camera; he's hanging out with the others, listening to Prince and asking him questions, sometimes from detailed notes he holds in his hand. He's a director attempting to shape an improvised performance into some kind of narrative coherence. It's the role of interviewer we see him perform in *The Last Waltz* but this time to greater effect. *American Boy* describes the process of making a documentary while *The Last Waltz* is the finished product.

The film opens in a desultory fashion and only very gradually begins to attain focus. When Prince enters the Hollywood home of George Memmoli, he engages in a wrestling struggle with Memmoli that goes on for about five minutes, then tells a series of unrelated stories. He's slowly prompted by questions from Scorsese and Memmoli to talk about his life as road manager for Neil Diamond and the heavy heroin addiction he developed. The mood is not confessional and repentant; it's often raw and humorous, as when he describes shooting up right after a bust by the cops, or sitting down on a fellow addict in the dim light of a shooting gallery. The stories here seem practiced, even rehearsed, and give rise to the idea that the notes Scorsese is holding were taken during earlier run-throughs. The problem of insufficiently controlled improvisation presents itself again.

The film does seem to come together in two final contrasting passages. The first involves Prince's horrific story of killing a robber during his rehabilitation from drugs. He's working in a gas station, the robber charges him with a knife, and Prince shoots him once in the chest at which point he falls back half dead, landing "between ethyl and regular." This is Prince's practiced joke line. He then empties the five remaining shots from what he describes as a .44 Magnum (the largest of Travis' gun purchases) into the robber. During this part of the narration Prince actually produces a gun and demonstrates his actions. He says he doesn't remember firing the five shots. This episode is described almost cinematically: the robber's glazed eyes and sweat-drenched face as he lunges forward are luridly rendered. It's a rehearsed performance and yet it has the same out-of-control, death-driven momentum as Travis' final eruption in *Taxi Driver*.

The second and final passage is very different. Under Scorsese's prompting, Prince gives three different versions of a phone call he makes to his parents. In the first he says his father asks if he enjoys making movies in Hollywood and he says, "Yes." Scorsese says this is too pat, too "thrown away." He wants to know the parents' reactions. Prince then says his mother is pleased that he likes his work, that his father is dying and that "I have a very hard time talking to him on the phone." In the third version, Prince begins by clicking his fingers and framing part of his face with his hands. It's as if he's saying, "We'll do the take now," after two rehearsals. There's a cut to the mobile camera and a light above it (the only time we see the camera) and then Prince repeats that he's happy in his work but this time in a very calm, even melancholy way. The performance veneer has been stripped away.

This passage stands in marked contrast to the killing of the robber. Scorsese's interventions get Prince to stop acting and to be more real. He's deconstructing Prince's desire to turn every story into a performance, which he as a member of the audience has in part encouraged. This is a vivid glimpse of Scorsese's skill as a director of actors and as a director making a film about creating a documentary.

Notes

1. *Scorsese on Scorsese*, 72.
2. Ibid., 72.
3. Ibid., 73.

Chapter 6

BLOODROPE

RAGING BULL, 1980

Raging Bull is probably Scorsese's greatest film. It is easy to see why he and scriptwriter Paul Schrader were attracted to the book of the same title by Jake LaMotta. LaMotta's book is a vivid, well-told story of guilt, punishment, and redemption in the world of boxing. As a young street-tough, LaMotta believes he's murdered a man for money. His guilt drives him to self-destructive acts in the ring, which involve the receiving and dealing out of punishment. He betrays his best friend, Pete, and then, much later, welcomes a beating Pete gives him at their reunion. The note of final absolution through suffering is much clearer in the book than in the film. De Niro gave Scorsese the book and pressed the project from the beginning. Scorsese has said that he and De Niro took Schrader's script and completely revised it, with De Niro making a majority of the contributions.[1] The film is the best example of collaboration at the script stage (LaMótta, Schrader, Scorsese, De Niro) in all of Scorsese's work. It's also the best example of Scorsese's cinematic expressionism.

Raging Bull is the finest boxing film ever made and yet, in a fundamental sense, it is not about boxing at all. Like the book, it is about LaMotta's spiritual journey. True to Scorsese's heroes, who are always men, LaMotta is compulsive, obsessional and violent. Acting out his frustrations and rages, he inflicts himself on others, loses their love and affection, and finds himself alone. From this low point he has the choice of death or rebirth. It's a "Pilgrim's Progress" set in the ring. The sources of LaMotta's rage are carefully suggested. His macho toughness is based in part on a fear of being feminine. He tells his brother, Joey (the film's version of Pete), "I got small hands like girl hands." And he makes a series of jokes and curses about anal intercourse between men. In the most prominent of these, he tells the godfather, Tommy Como, what he's going to do to the handsome, beautiful young fighter, Tony Janeiro, in an upcoming bout: "I'm going to open his hole up like this [making the gesture of a wide orifice with his hands]. I don't know whether I should fuck him or fight him." The homoerotic element here is presented in terms of the domination of one man by another. The beaten fighter is feminized; a winning fighter is always sure of his masculinity. The lack of integration of the feminine in a man who participates in a violent sport makes LaMotta especially dangerous, most of all to himself. As his remarks to Como suggest, he's completely uncensored—even Como's hardened henchmen are surprised by the crack about fucking Janeiro. His extremism will take him all the way down into darkness, and ultimately toward the light.

This extremism is seen best in Jake's need to receive blows, as well as give them. Immediately after a fight with his first wife, he instructs Joey to hit him in the face. His face is still raw from a recent fight against Jimmie Reeves, which he lost. After receiving several insults and slaps ("Your mother takes it in the ass"; "What are you, a lady?"), Joey obliges and reopens Jake's cuts. He's still furious with his loss to Reeves and with his wife, but he is also judgmentally angry at himself and seeks punishment. In the moments after his second loss to Robinson, it is Joey who destroys a locker room chair while Jake seems contemplative: "I've done a lot of bad things, Joey; maybe it's coming back to me." He's aware of his fate coming toward him in the form of blows, that his rage is a form of sleep, and that truth—waking up—comes in blows.

Another source of LaMotta's rage is his pathological jealousy about his second wife, Vickie. The book makes the source of this jealousy abundantly clear in LaMotta's brave admission that he experienced prolonged episodes of sexual impotency with Vickie. For some reason, Schrader chose to omit this fact from the script; the result is that LaMotta's suspicions that Vickie is sleeping with every man she comes in contact with take on a more purely irrational character. We can't locate the cause of these fantasies; all we see is that LaMotta has a very short fuse. We don't see that his rage is impotent rage, born of frustration and humiliation. The unbelievably savage beating he gives Janeiro are caused by Vickie's offhand remark that Janeiro is "a good-looking guy." All the men he attacks with such frenzy in the ring are Vickie's lovers because he is not her lover.

One can only wonder why Schrader, De Niro, and Scorsese omitted LaMotta's impotence. Did they calculate that such references would prevent male identification with the hero (it's alright to be wildly aggressive, but not alright to experience impotence)? If so, such an omission says a great deal about the conventional concept of maleness. In this sense, LaMotta's book is more courageous than Scorsese's film—but not a better work of art.

The references we do have in the film to LaMotta's sexuality suggest that he consciously controls his sex with Vickie to serve his endurance in the ring. Like Floyd Patterson and countless other fighters—and unlike Ingemar Johansson, who brought his mistress to training camp—he is a celibate before a fight. In a strong sequence before the third fight with Sugar Ray Robinson, LaMotta instructs Vickie how to seduce him. As she moves her mouth down his body, toward his penis, he becomes wild with desire and rushes into the bathroom where a pitcher of ice-crammed water conveniently awaits him. He pours it over his genitals as he mutters to Vickie, who amorously pursues him, that "if I fight Robinson, I can't fool around." In a sense, he's using Vickie to key himself up for the fight. The implications of this comic scene are far removed from the poignancy of impotence.

Another way in which LaMotta, for all his craziness, is made to be sympathetic lies in his opposition to the mob. He won't let the godfather and his cronies control his career—that is, until he finally perceives that he'll never get a title shot unless he cooperates. He's the proud little guy resisting the pressures of powerful institutions. This cliché has been trotted out in too many American films to mention, particularly in cop films. It is a staple myth of our popular culture and is usually treated in a hackneyed

fashion. Scorsese gives freshness to it by making it real: LaMotta isn't out
to reform anybody; he doesn't want the mob to get the money he fights for.
Moreover, he's intensely jealous of Sal, one of Tommy Como's lieuten-
ants, who has a special interest in Vickie. Sal is a dapper fellow, with an
empty face. He's often shot in partial slow motion, putting on his glasses,
lighting a cigarette with a carefully stylized gesture. He is Mr. Smooth,
who looks good in the Copacabana nightclub and always says the right
things to "Mr. Como." We share the hard-working LaMotta's contempt for
him. Sal will reappear in more distorted, comic, and threatening forms in
Goodfellas.

Joey, LaMotta's brother, stands in particularly equivocal relationship
to Sal and the mob. As LaMotta's manager he sees, before Jake does, that
they'll eventually have to give in. He's intensely loyal to Jake, yet he
doesn't mind associating with Como; part of him buys into the godfather
culture. He's like Charlie in *Mean Streets*, inside and outside at the same
time. He puts up with Jake's abuse because he loves him. His attack on Sal
in the Copacabana is even wilder than one of Jake's fights. He is acting as
Jake would act in discovering Vickie at the nightclub with Sal, except that
Jake would also beat up Vickie. He acts out of family loyalty; he's also
Jake's last connection (besides Vickie) to another human being. When
Jake attacks him after Vickie, fed to the teeth with Jake's jealousy, says
she "sucked his cock and all the other cocks on the street," Jake loses his
main source of support and his life turns sharply down. Joey is also the
main agent of Jake's rebirth. Their pained reunion toward the end of the
film marks the start of Jake's upward movement. In the hands of Joe Pesci,
Joey is convincingly the sane, loyal, adoring brother—the only person who
can talk sense to Jake and get away with it. He's not without his own
irrational violence, however; he tells his little son at the kitchen table that
he'll stick a knife in him if he doesn't use his knife and fork properly. He
is "Charlie" to De Niro's "Johnny Boy."

Vickie, as played by Cathy Moriarty in a stunning performance, is the
perfect foil to Jake's edgy turbulence. She's languid, slow, beautiful,
passive, soft at the edges, with a street-smart coarseness when she needs
it. Somehow she is able to put up with Jake's jealous rages and his
determination to keep her out of circulation. Perhaps it's because, despite
all of his aggressive strength and achievement, she's the one with the
power in their relationship. He consistently comes to her calm strength,
looking for comfort and grace. Twenty years younger than Jake and
possessing no special maternal qualities, she is still a mother to him.

In spite of Pesci's and Moriarty's fine performances, it is still possible to imagine others doing their roles. This isn't true for De Niro's "Jake," one of the indelible performances of our time. Jake is a predictable person in his compulsions, yet he's not without cunning and deviousness and intelligence. As a fighter he was famous for faking weariness or injury, and then surprising his opponent with his brutality (the film's brief evocation of the Dauthauille fight captures this). The progress of Jake's career from colorful fighter to successful nightclub entertainer (the ex-pug as literary clown) is a vivid one. In many ways the role is about acting as much as fighting, and De Niro evokes these multiple roles with astonishing authenticity. The "fat" scenes in the nightclubs and dressing rooms, which bracket the main narration, are perhaps even more convincing than the fight scenes—superb as they are. De Niro isn't merely carrying a fat body (his weight gain has become the most renowned aspect of his performance): his soul is fat, congealed, heavy with self-indulgence and remorse. This inner state is best seen in the cheap bar where Jake introduces a stripper, who isn't exactly young, and then exchanges insults with the bored customers, telling one he'd like to piss in his drink. Perhaps De Niro had to get fat to really feel the role. In any case, the evocation of LaMotta's metamorphosis through a variety of physical and spiritual states (eager young fighter, jealous husband and father, self-indulgent champion, bloated nightclub owner, jailed convict, successful entertainer) is unforgettable. The underlying idea is endurance: LaMotta is the guy who won't go down in the ring ("You never got me down, Ray"), who never gives up on life, who continued—long after the immortal Robinson was dead!—to live on.

In cinematic terms, the film functions in the two basic modes which by now have become Scorsese trademarks: a documentary-like realism and expressionism. The documentary is used to describe LaMotta outside the ring, the expressionistic inside the ring. We see the extreme realism of one mode in the "home movie" sequence, which Scorsese uses to foreshorten the period during which Jake marries Vickie, they have kids, and he pursues his victorious career. Many other sequences have this same documentary feeling: when Jake first sees Vickie at the pool; when he takes her, for the first time, to the family home; the discussion at the kitchen table before the Janeiro fight; and the sequence right after Jake has won the title, in which he and Joey discuss how to fix the TV. In each of these sequences, there's an off-hand, desultory quality to the dialogue, and the camera moves relatively little and shoots in long takes. It's as if we are watching an unrehearsed enactment of these people's lives. In part, this quality is achieved through Scorsese's success at keeping his actors' improvisations within a defined format. There doesn't seem to be much artifice at work but, of course, there is.

As an example of the film's documentary-like realism, I want to look briefly at the eight-shot sequence in which Jake brings Vickie to his parents' home for the first time. His mom and dad aren't home, so the new friends move from room to room as Jake shows her around. There's very little dialogue, a great deal of unspoken attraction between them, and a good deal of comedy in their initial awkwardness: Jake takes her into the dining room and tells her it's the dining room, and then he points to a bird cage and says, "It's a bird . . . or was a bird. It died, I think." The most interesting shots are the three longest: 40, 62, and 105 seconds, respectively. In the sixth shot (62 seconds), for instance, Scorsese has them sitting at opposite ends of a table; Jake tells Vickie she's too far away and to move closer, and she eventually winds up on his lap. They are shot in middle distance, Jake in profile and Vickie with her back to the camera part of the time. There's no attempt to charm, manipulate, or seduce the audience by cutting in close-up from face to face, by having them speak romantic dialogue reinforced by romantic music; instead, someone is singing in Italian on a distant radio. The camera holds on them, keeping them at a distance as they tentatively act out their attraction. There's no buildup, no crescendo or false intensification to this and the other shots in the sequence. It's as if we are quiet observers standing across the room, watching a natural exchange take place. The eighth and longest shot has the same effect. They go into the bedroom and sit down on the bed; Vickie gets up to look at a photo of Jake and Joey on the chest of drawers; Jake starts kissing her, and they move offscreen left as the camera closes on the photo. Almost nothing is said in this nearly two-minute shot, and yet a significant transaction has taken place in a relaxed, down-to-earth rhythm. The whole sequence has the reality of everyday existence. The documentary and expressionistic are not discrete modes, of course. The TV fixing sequence turns into Jake's wild attack on Joey when he's having dinner with his family. At first Jake and Joey discuss how to adjust the TV and the atmosphere in the small living room is like a home movie. But Jake has other things on his mind and his jealousy eventually goads him to ask Joey, "Did you fuck my wife?" Scorsese says that he wrote seven pages of dialogue for this, "the only full-length dialogue scene in the film."[2] De Niro's obsessional behavior emerges slowly from the random exchanges about the TV. Vickie's angry response to his accusations ("I fucked all of them . . . I sucked your brother's cock") propels Jake into Joey's family dinner. The attack is filmed like the boxing sequences, with fast cutting, tilt frames, and even some of the sound effects of the fights. Joey is knocked to the floor then through a glass door as the women try to drag Jake away. Jake then slugs Vickie.

It is the boxing sequences which show Scorsese at his creative, experimental best and give *Raging Bull* its special power. Many boxing films have taken the camera in the ring and moved it around with athletic quickness, but no fight film I know captures the brutality of the sport in the delirious, nightmarish way which Scorsese achieves. It's as if the fights were shot by Hieronymus Bosch or Celine. Scorsese's expressionism in these sequences speaks to the irrational, the ungoverned, the dreamlike, unmediated drives in all of us. It is deeply disturbing stuff—not the bloody, macho entertainment of a good fight film like *Champion* (Kirk Douglas). It strikes through fantasies of male domination directly into chaos, horror, death. It is the difference between seeing a tough fight from the upper rows of the balcony or on a sanitized TV presentation and being in the front rows where you can get spattered with blood. Scorsese wants to suck you into the vortex, not leave you at a distance. The sequences of everyday realism, such as Jake and Vickie's visit to his parents' home, function to give the fight sequences their power by way of contrast. The film has the chronological structure of a standard biography, with the Robinson fights as the "main events," carefully led up to, and their aftermath carefully noticed as well. The fight sequences are designed to build up to the fifth and last Robinson fight, which is presented as a culmination of LaMotta's rage and self-punishment.

We first get a sense of what Scorsese is up to in the Jimmie Reeves fight sequence. The riot that follows the decision in favor of Reeves is filmed relatively straightforwardly—except for a wild floor-level shot of a woman being trampled in the stampede near the ring. In the first Robinson fight, expressionistic devices begin to appear in the sound of wind (an approaching storm) and in the use of silence. In part, Scorsese is working with sound distortions as the fighters might experience them in the ring. LaMotta's knockdown of Robinson in the second fight, the only fight with Robinson he wins, is presented with some wonderful, fast cutting—particularly a lightning-fast shot in bright, flashbulb light of Robinson lying outside the ropes. As with all the fight sequences, except the last Robinson fight, the presentation is extremely brief and elliptical.

In the Janeiro fight, many shots are almost too fast to count. Blood leaps from Janeiro's face, accompanied by a spurting, gushing sound and the sound of a windstorm. As Janeiro goes down for the last time, in partial slow motion, the camera rotates over in time with his fall. The effect is to put the viewer into the fall—and the blood, in a visceral way. Many other fight sequences begin like a blow in the face: a quiet, domestic scene explodes into the noise and motion of ring violence. The Cerdan fight is framed by conventional TV or movie images of touching gloves and numbers of rounds, but within these standard details Scorsese shows both fighters in tilt frame, water from the cornerman's sponge running down their bodies. These are evocative images of exhaustion.

After LaMotta's assault on his brother, and his continued rejection of him later in an attempted phone call, the expressionistic effects intensify. The high point of boxing violence is connected to the high point of his domestic violence, as Jake acts out his fate in the ring. This pattern is most clearly seen in the fifth and last Robinson fight—a masterful sequence of about fifty shots, and the best example of the film's cinematic brilliance. The first seven shots use water running down Jake's body from a soaked sponge to suggest exhaustion, as in the Cerdan fight. But this time the water is dark with blood. In shot eight we see a TV image of LaMotta in his corner as a Pabst beer ad comes on. Joey and his wife are watching the fight. In shot 18 the fighters are in the thirteenth round and Robinson punches LaMotta at will. In shot 19, LaMotta stands at the ropes and yells at Robinson to come on. He's repeating, in an extreme form, his demand to Joey to hit him. In 20, Robinson gets ready to punch as the camera pulls away and down, and the roar of the crowd diminishes to silence. There is a low sound of a building, roaring storm. As Robinson advances toward the camera in shot 24, the roar rises. The sequence then explodes into about ten lightning shots in which Robinson punishes LaMotta, blood spurts from Jake's face, there's the sound of clacking machinery as the crowd screams and moans (or is it wind?), and Vickie buries her face in her hands. Suddenly there's a relatively low, slow shot of Robinson raising his fist to deliver the final blow. Strangely, the fist is held high above his head in a position no good fighter would use to deliver a punch. His stance is like an iconographic representation of divine punishment—the hand of God about to deliver justice. As he starts the blow, the roar of windstorm intensifies, the blow falls on LaMotta, blood spatters the ringsides, Vickie bends down into her hands, Jake stands with a bloodied, bowed head, and the fight is stopped as the TV commentator says that row after row of spectators are standing and cheering Robinson's victory and LaMotta's courage. We see Joey's painful reaction to Jake's beating and, in shot 45, LaMotta's crazy taunt to Robinson, "You never got me down, Ray," as Robinson's cornermen laugh at him. The sequence ends with what is, for me, the finest shot in the film: at the sound of the bell, the camera shows an empty, neutral corner, then pans slowly to the right, picking up the ring announcer as he comes through the ropes, noticing Robinson's cornermen as they celebrate, moves along the strand of ring rope until the announcer proclaims Robinson the winner, and it comes to rest on a place where the rope is gashed and "bleeding." The "bleeding rope" is the culmination of Scorsese's expressionist images. It is important to point out that the rope is bleeding; there isn't simply blood on the rope. It's an image out of the vortex of violence we've just been through.[3]

A couple of additional comments on the fight sequences need to be made. First, there's only one false note: when LaMotta pulls back a punch at the bell in the Reeves fight. LaMotta, a brawler, didn't do that kind of thing. Second, actual footage of the last Robinson fight shows that LaMotta was nearly unmarked at the end. Leading with his huge head, willing to take two hard shots so that he could hook to the body, he nevertheless didn't cut easily. In the jargon of the trade, he was a "catcher" but not a "bleeder." The bloodiness of Scorsese's sequences is poetic license artfully used.

There's also a verbal context to the fight sequences which is nearly as important as the visual. Using the voice of the great blow-by-blow commentator, Don Dunphy, Scorsese fills us in on the progress of LaMotta's career, as well as gives us vivid descriptions which enhance the images. Radio descriptions, we must remember, were mainly the way the public experienced important fights in the '40s and early '50s. The use of the actual sound track of Ted Husing's commentary on the last Robinson fight is particularly effective. Exhaustive effort was made to portray the way boxing was presented to the public in LaMotta's historical moment, as well as to portray what life was like in the subculture of boxing at that time. The careful attribution in the credits to specific fighters in specific fight sequences attests to Scorsese's efforts at authenticity. The fights outside the ring aren't filmed the same way as the fights in the ring. Joey's attack on Sal at the Copacabana, bashing him again and again with the car door, is filmed with conventional realism. The decision to shoot with black and white film stock was partially based on the way TV and newsreels, in the earliest days, presented boxing.

Finally, there's the nearly miraculous editing of the fight sequences. Scorsese has said that when he looked at the raw footage of the fight sequences, he felt that the film was a total chaos, a madhouse. His work in meticulous editing, along with Thelma Schoonmaker, is one of the best examples of his shaping artistry in film. Frank Warner's sound effects are also brilliant in the fight sequences. He used melons breaking, rifle shots, storm sounds among many others. The sound mixing took sixteen weeks and was nearly as complicated as the editing—and certainly as important in achieving expressionist effects.

A final question remains about *Raging Bull*. How much does Jake really change at the end of the movie? LaMotta's book, as I've suggested, asserts a clear, unambiguous redemption which the epigraph to the film echoes in the biblical quote about the man who was once blind but can now see. The movie itself—more implacable in its realism, less attuned to the myths of popular culture—is more cautious. Jake has received blows, has suffered, but has he experienced spiritual redemption in the process? He is not a religious figure in any sense. The reunion with Joey is tentative; Joey receives Jake's aggressive hugs and kisses with a stiffened body, though he says two or three times, in response to Jake's insistences, that he'll phone him. The tenderness Jake displays here, immediately after insulting the bar customers, is the only evidence we have of deeper change. The Barbizon Hotel, where Jake is performing works by Shakespeare, Chayevsky, and Tennessee Williams, is certainly a step up from the sleazy bar. In the final shot, an overweight Jake, this time in a tux, rehearses his lines with enthusiasm and calls himself "champ" as he goes into one of his boxing warmups. It's the very beginning of the long way back.[4]

The power of *Raging Bull* comes from Scorsese's life as well as his artistry. After the commercial failure of *New York, New York*, Scorsese, a severe asthmatic, began using drugs in earnest and wound up in the hospital. He agreed to do the film, after initial reservations, when he felt he could use LaMotta's self-destructiveness to take a good look at his own. Like all his best work, the film came out of his guts. It's dedication is particularly moving: "To Haig P. Manoogian, teacher, 1916–1980. With love and resolution, Marty." Manoogian, the teacher at NYU who first introduced Scorsese to film work, did not live long enough to see the completed film. The "resolution" is Scorsese's statement that, like LaMotta, he won't go down, that he'll rededicate himself to making films. It is a religious dedication.

Notes

1. *Scorsese on Scorsese*, 76-77.

2. Ibid., 83.

3. The origin of this shot comes from Scorsese's witness in Madison Square Garden: "I was in the fifth row from the front, and I saw blood coming off the rope. As the next bout was announced, no one took any notice of it." *Scorsese on Scorsese*, 80.

4. Scorsese's comment that "Jake LaMotta acted much tougher in real life than he appeared in the film" is worth noting. *Scorsese on Scorsese*, 78.

Chapter 7

EMPTY SPACES

THE KING OF COMEDY, 1983

The King of Comedy was probably Scorsese's most keenly anticipated film. Word that he was using Jerry Lewis and De Niro in his first full-length comedy added to the expectation. When the film appeared, it did well for awhile in a few big cities but sank like a stone elsewhere. The audience, expecting pleasurable laughter, was put off by its harshness. It didn't seem to be a comedy at all. In fact, in its examination of our celebrity culture, *The King of Comedy* is one of the best black comedies of our time—on a par with *Cul de Sac* and *The Tenant*, masterpieces by the king of black comedies, Roman Polanski.

The film is based on a novel by Paul Zimmerman which examines the zaniness of celebrity worship. De Niro read Zimmerman's script of the novel and, having purchased it, pressed it on Scorsese. De Niro evidently liked the bizarre central character, Rupert Pupkin—his oddball cheerfulness, his determination not to be a nobody. According to Scorsese, De Niro himself reworked the script extensively.[1] Like *Raging Bull,* the film can be said to be as much De Niro's as Scorsese's or Zimmerman's. It is one of his finest performances—on a par with *Raging Bull*—though it's a performance all in one key.

The story is fairly straightforward. Rupert Pupkin, who collects autographs of celebrities, develops a fixation on the talk-show host, Jerry Langford. In fact, he believes that he is Langford, or a replication of him, since he conducts talk-show monologues with cardboard cutout celebrities in the basement of his mother's house. He invades Langford's privacy, extracting a promise that a tape of one of his routines will be listened to. He can't see that he's politely being put off and that he'll never get on Langford's show. As his frustration grows, he combines with Masha, another celebrity nut, to kidnap Langford and blackmail his way onto the show. As the result of his crime and TV notoriety, he becomes a media celebrity, serves a sentence of two-and-a-half years, publishes an autobiography, and becomes an entertainer.

The violence of the first extended scene in the film warns immediately that we're not witnessing an ordinary comedy. We're shoved into a crowd waiting for Langford to exit the network studio. These celebrity freaks all know each other. They greet Rupert asking, "Who'd you get today, Rupe?" (whose autograph). He responds in a blasé fashion, "It's not my whole life; it should be, but it isn't." This assertion is quickly contradicted in the riot which ensues. In a horrifying sequence, Masha manages to force her way into Langford's limo and drives him out into the tumultuous crowd where Rupert assumes the role of his protector. Rupert reenters the limo with Langford and cheerfully insists that Langford invite him on the show. He won't take "No" for an answer, and he won't let Langford go when they reach his apartment. He makes a joke about showing Jerry his pride and joy and produces pictures of the detergents "Pride" and "Joy." This sequence suggests that Rupert has no sense of humor, that he is essentially harmless, just incredibly pushy. All of these assumptions are wrong. When it isn't canned, his humor can be quite good, though of the aggressive variety: he tells Langford, after he has brought his girlfriend Rita uninvited to Langford's country house, "Look, Jerry, we set up a story where you invite all your friends out for a weekend and then throw them all in jail." In dramatic context, this is a funny line. It also reveals what Zimmerman has called Rupert's "ability to transform reality through language."[2] He acts as if he's in control of the situation. "What's your pleasure, Jerry?" he says when Langford, astounded, walks into his home. His words suggest that he is the host. He'd like to hear Langford ask the question of him, so he says it. He's both Langford and Rupert at this moment, as in his basement. He's funny but delusional. Like a fiction writer, he lives in his inventions.

The film's three major fantasy sequences have an increasingly imperative quality and lead up to the kidnapping. In the first, Langford pleads with Rupert to go on the show, while they're having lunch at Sardi's. In the second, he raves at Rupert about the high quality of his comedy routines, shaking him roughly in his enthusiasm and mauling his face with his hands (a slapstick element we see at other times in the film). The last and longest fantasy sequence has Rupert as a guest in a "this-is-your-life format," with Langford presiding. His old high school principal tells Rupert that they all didn't think he'd amount to anything, "but we were wrong and, Rupert, you were right . . . We'd like to apologize to you personally before the entire nation and to beg your forgiveness for all the things we did to you . . . We'd like to thank you personally for the meaning you've given our lives" (wild applause which nevertheless sounds canned). The increasingly compulsive self-validation in these sequences approaches a kind of megalomania. A little is not enough: everything must be inflated. That these fantasies occur at moments of rejection—when Rupert is waiting endlessly in the network offices, when Langford puts him off as he enters his apartment—isn't surprising. They are retreats from painful reality, like Rupert's basement setup where he can conduct his own talk shows free of every interruption, save his mother's voice.

The beauty of De Niro's performance is that he manages to make the bizarre and obsessive likeable. His Rupert is like a windup toy, full of bows, head-cocking, smirking, reflexively adjusting his tie—in constant motion and talking all the time in the sugary vocal mannerisms of an overpolite salesperson. He is indefatigable. We never see him at rest or in a relaxed posture. When he sits, it is usually in a symmetrical posture, feet close together, hands folded in his lap. His gestures are often symmetrical as well and stiff as if programmed; he feels no comfort in his body. He's a good boy who minds his mother when she yells at him ("Ma'am, puh-lease stop calling me," he responds with a childlike inflection). A central part of him has not gone beyond his childhood. His basement "studio" is like a playhouse. He dresses neatly in a kind of oddball leisure style—red pants, white shoes. The masterful grooming touch, undoubtedly concocted by De Niro, is Rupert's hair, which appears to be a black, mildly greased wig with a slight pompadour and bouffant fullness. You can tell he is vain (read self-engrossed) about his appearance, especially his hair. He's a young man (actually approaching middle age) from a working-class family who's on his way up in the world. He is very interested in decorum. In this aspect he's not far removed from Travis Bickle, but without the overt rage. He becomes uneasy when Rita starts drinking Langford's liquor, dancing and running upstairs to see Langford's bedroom.

His compatriot, Masha, is the complementary figure, the unrepressed side of his weirdness. She's younger, in her early twenties, and still dresses in the uniform of a prep school student—white socks, blazer with coat-of-arms. Her language reveals that she, too, is located in childhood. Referring to Langford, she speaks in the language of the schoolyard, "When he's got a gun on him, all of a sudden he wants to make up and be friends." Her parents may be rich, but she's been equally neglected. Celebrity worship cuts across all classes. She's upper class (perhaps she went to Chapin or Brierly), unkempt, and totally uncensored. Her monologue to the bound-and-gagged Langford, like Rupert's later TV monologue, is full of reference to an abused childhood. Her violence and aggression are horrifying in the opening sequence. When Langford spots her following him in the street, he runs. She and Rupert are competitors in their obsession with Langford, often meeting in the street to find out who's had the most success in getting his attention. In the kidnap scene she's full of wild sexual energy, while Rupert hardly has any sexual interest in his love obsession, the gorgeous Rita. As played by Sandra Bernhard, Masha is a nightmare figure. The anger and aggression that lie deep beneath Rupert's sugary, repressed surface are fully enacted by her. She's the tip-off that Rupert isn't essentially harmless.

When Rupert finally does his monologue on the Langford show, it's full of references to his painful childhood: "My parents were too poor to afford me a childhood . . . they made two down payments on me, but also returned me to the hospital as defective." He says that his parents were both alcoholic, and that when his father hit him "it was the only attention he ever gave me." The other kids beat him up all the time. He grew up thinking that throwing up (from too much alcohol) "was a sign of maturity." "My only interest was show business. I began at the top collecting autographs" (this last joke draws a hearty—canned?—laugh). These lines are delivered with Rupert's characteristically stiff, symmetrical gestures. He has overrehearsed. Still, there's enthusiasm, hopefulness, and even euphoria in this appearance on national TV. "It's better to be a king for a night than a schmuck for a lifetime," he says. He's a nobody trying to make it big, and the audience goes out of their way to support him. His one-liners aren't that witty, however. The laughter seems forced, canned, or both. His big comic moment is only partially funny. It's a comedy full of pain and sorrow. It is surprising that there's not more overt anger and aggression in it. The anger is in the event, the kidnapping: "Jerry can't be here because he's tied up. I tied him; that's the only way I could get on this show." This is both a confession and a declaration of his need for a moment of celebrityhood, which the film assumes we all share to some degree. In his *Acting in the Cinema* James Naremore devotes a full chapter to *The King of Comedy*, in which he argues that celebrityhood and role playing permeate the film, "foregrounding the work of performers and playfully undermining every form of behavioral sincerity."[3]

The King of Comedy examines the increasingly close association in modern comedy between comedy and anger. Gone are the days of Bob Hope and Jack Benny. Today's comedy is increasingly *ad hominem*, a blow against a person, group, or idea. No subject matter is out of bounds, no extremes of language barred. Insult comics like Don Rickles abound. The comedian has merged with the performance artist, resulting in monologues of disturbing invention. Sandra Bernhard, a performance artist herself, is an excellent example. In this sense, like any artist, Rupert is using his pain to make a series of forays into the past. He can't get beyond his past, however; he can't break through to an awakened, stronger state like Scorsese's other heroes. He is the same at the end as he is at the beginning, and this accounts for the necessity of De Niro's one-key performance. He's the nicest but also the strangest of Scorsese's antisocial heroes. In part, Rupert's inability to change is the result of his fixation on a traumatized past, but in another sense he's trapped in the ethos of celebrity worship and performance in which the only value lies in the ephemeral fifteen minutes of so-called fame. We don't know what his work is; he seems to have no job, no existence which might serve to remove him momentarily from his fantasies and confront him with the opportunity to do a mundane task. Cut loose from ordinary life, he has become a caricature, a creature of the manipulations of television. Television is the operative visual mode in the film from the brief opening sequence in which the frame is filled with the opening of the Jerry Langford show, to Rupert's fantasy marriage to Rita, to his actual appearance on the show. Many dialogue scenes are shot in medium close-up, with the usual talking heads effect. Unlike so many films which seem designed to be shown on TV more than in the theater, *The King of Comedy* uses these images to suggest television's power in our celebrity-driven culture. Rupert has a TV show running constantly in his head.

The central shot in the film occurs fairly early, just after the first basement scene. Immediately after Rupert's mom yells down, we see a medium closeup of Rupert's back: he's facing a large still photograph of a laughing audience, while the soundtrack gives us their canned laughter. The camera slowly backs away as the laughter intensifies into distortion, and we see Rupert standing at the end of a long corridor, the gleaming walls and ceilings of which are increasingly emphasized as the shot comes to a close. It's an inside shot which perfectly evokes his self-enclosure. The spareness of the shot—the absence of variegated surfaces—is quite like the look of much of the film. This corridor shot isn't like the shots when Rita walks into the narrow, dingy hall of her apartment while Rupert cheerily waves good-bye. Rita's halls are the real world.

Scorsese has said that in making *The King of Comedy* he wanted to use a plain style, unlike the bravura camera work of *Raging Bull*. Such a style was well calculated to evoke the emptiness which lies behind Rupert's constant activity. It is the visual equivalent of the void that surrounds his laughter in the basement or in his other fantasies, since no one else hears it. Scorsese's cutting is particularly effective here: he'll show us Rupert and Langford, for instance, laughing at one of Rupert's jokes, then cut on the fantasy laughter to show us Rupert laughing alone. The camera often shoots Rupert head-on, particularly when he's in one of his symmetrical postures. The decor of many environments is very plain as well, if not empty. The waiting room at the network offices where Rupert spends so much of his time has a number of blank, off-white walls, no indoor plants, no artwork. The space has been intentionally designed to suggest vacancy, sterility, the impersonal. It nicely evokes Rupert's condition. In this sense, Scorsese's plain style functions to capture Rupert's inner world. The whole film becomes a product of that world. As an example, we have an interesting shot directly after Jerry Langford's assistant Miss Long tells Rupert his demo tape isn't good enough. Rather than leave, Rupert sits down and waits to see Langford. He's on the far right of the frame, the receptionist on the far left and in the middle a plain blank corner of the room. The shot lasts sixteen seconds and our eyes are drawn inevitably to the space of the corner. It's the dead end Rupert refuses to acknowledge but which he feels when he tells the receptionist on another occasion that he's like the man who waited so long he forgot what he came for. The lighting in this shot as in many other interiors has the monotone uniformity of a TV production.

Another example of a subjective/objective shot is the last one in the film. Dressed in a red suit and his standard white shoes, Rupert stands in the spotlight of a large nightclub receiving applause from an ecstatic audience while an announcer's smarmy voice milks them for greater response. He bows and smirks, the waves of applause grow louder and louder as the camera closes in. It's an inflated parody of the opening of any late-night talk show on TV. The shot tells us that Rupert has become a successful performer but its inflation also suggests that it's from within Rupert's fantasy—a reverse of the earlier gleaming corridor shot where he's photographed from the rear.

Interestingly, Langford's apartment is equally anonymous—full of cold, reflective metal and glass surfaces. A single television is always on. He sits down to eat alone at a glass table, though he has told Rupert he's having guests. There's a curious sense of connection between Langford and Rupert here. Langford, in fact, is almost always seen alone—even more than Rupert or Masha. We don't see him with his coworkers; he always walks to lunch alone. He's at his country house alone. The successful comedian, as well as the unsuccessful, are visually situated in aloneness.[4] Langford's country home is almost equally spare. There are no rugs on the hardwood floors, the white walls have few artworks. It's like an art gallery, not a space one might feel at home in, though it does have natural light and one can see trees out the windows. It is the absence of comfort in these environments that connects so well to our sense of Rupert's own lack of comfort in himself. Langford's choice of a spare environment, it should be added, may well function as an antidote to the crowded, tumultuous life of a TV talk show host.

Rupert's eventual success as a performer—after the thirty months in jail, which he uses "to sharpen his material"—is like Travis Bickle's success at the end of *Taxi Driver*. Each achieves notoriety as the result of a criminal act. The acting out of their antisocial impulses is misconstrued, in Travis' case, as heroism and as just a gutsy effort at a show business breakthrough in Rupert's. The public's need for constant distraction may lie at the heart of Travis' and Rupert's successes. They are like momentary blips on the screen, images in the endless stream which make up our popular culture. In De Niro's wonderful performance, Rupert is both strange and familiar. He is like we are when, standing in the supermarket checkout line, we idly pick up *People* magazine to read about a celebrity that interests us. He has merely pushed the identification further.

Notes

1. Mary Pat Kelly, *Martin Scorsese: A Journey* (New York: Thunder's Mouth Press, 1991), 157.

2. Ibid., 159.

3. James Naremore, *Acting in the Cinema* (Berkeley: University of California Press, 1988), 263.

4. Though Robert Kolker doesn't treat *The King of Comedy*, it fits well with his thesis in *A Cinema of Loneliness* (New York: Oxford University Press, 1988).

Chapter 8

BAD LADIES

AFTER HOURS, 1985

After Hours was made after the last minute cancellation of shooting for *The Last Temptation of Christ*. Scorsese's rage and frustration threatened to undo him so he set about immediately to find a small budget project. *After Hours* was made for about four million dollars, a small sum at the time. The dismal commercial failure of *The King of Comedy* also provoked Scorsese to find a lighter, funnier vehicle. The film is often dismissed as a disappointment, but it is an entertaining, fast-paced nightmare comedy. *After Hours* is a "little" film, with a script by Joseph Minion. Griffin Dunne, the main actor, functioned as coproducer. The film tells the story of Paul Hacket's (Dunne) wild night in the Soho area of New York, during which he is unable to make his way home. We watch Paul move from his comfortable, boring workplace into the uncertain,

85

strange, and threatening world of the denizens of Soho lofts and club scenes. His increasing angst and paranoia are presented in comic terms. He returns to work in the early hours of the morning, flung out of a robber's van, encased in a papier-mâché sculpture which cracks open, leaving him to enter his office dirty and dusty, but glad to be back in the normal boring routine.

A summary of the many incidents of Paul's Soho experience would be overlong. He moves from one encounter to the next, increasingly frustrated by his inability to get home and sleep. He's lost his only money, a $20 bill which blows out the window during a wild cab ride. The crazed cab driver is his carrier to the underworld. The links between incidents are largely provided by a bizarre, and increasingly threatening, series of women who show an interest in him.

The opening sequence is worth a close look. A brisk section of Mozart's *Symphony K73* accompanies the camera behind the credits as it moves swiftly though the office where Paul works at his desk. This musical accompaniment seems an odd opening for a film about the nightmarish absurdities of contemporary life; it sounds as if the film is an older comedy of manners à la Renoir doing Beaumarchais. We are, in fact, going to experience a comedy of manners in modern Soho dress. The Soho art and club scenes are subjects of satire. As one burglar says to another (the actor is Cheech of Cheech and Chong fame), the uglier a work of art is the more expensive it is. In the office, Paul is instructing a new employee in the use of his computer, but he quickly loses interest when the employee informs him that he's only a temporary hire and that he has much larger plans to establish a magazine with real intellectual dimension. (We gather that Paul works in the publication area, possibly for a commercial magazine.) As Paul's attention drifts away from the voluble temp, we're given several close-up shots of female secretaries' hands performing clerical tasks. These aren't point-of-view shots from Paul, but shots reminding the viewer of the world of mundane work (performed entirely by women) of which Paul is a part. He is mildly bored in his job and irritated at the temp's idealism. He gets up from his desk and walks away while the temp is in mid-sentence. This rudeness is uncharacteristic of Paul. We come to see him as someone who usually tends to bend over backward when someone lays claim to his attention and his sympathies. Paul has settled for the ordinary, the routine. Is he irritated by the temp because he reminds him of his former idealistic self? We see him at home flipping through channels on his TV, lying on the couch, lonely, at loose ends.

The first woman who claims his attention is Marcie (Rosanna Arquette). She invites him down to Soho late that same night, after they've met in a coffee shop. But Marcie isn't there when Paul arrives. Her roommate Kiki (Linda Farentino) is working on a life-size papier-mâché sculpture of a crouching man whose face is in agony. Paul gives Kiki a shoulder rub and she goes to sleep, at which point Marcie shows up. In Marcie's bedroom, she accuses Paul ("What did you do to her?"). Paul's defensiveness is understandable. He doesn't know how to take Marcie. The attractive, friendly woman in the coffee shop is now alternately accusing, then giddy and giggling. Her story to Paul of being raped is a good example of the shifting reality Paul is experiencing. She tells him she was raped at knife point for six hours in the same bedroom they are now in (deep sympathy from Paul), then adds, "It was my boyfriend" and "I slept through most of it," ending with the casually dismissive "So there you are." While Marcie is speaking, she's dressed in a loose-fitting bathrobe and the camera glimpses some ambiguous markings on her upper thigh. Are they scratches, a tattoo? The purpose of this scene is to subject Paul's conventional responses to Marcie's weird changefulness. Thinking he's gone down to Soho for a very late date and possibly some sex, Paul is entering a world in which, as a diner owner later says, "Different rules apply when it gets this late. It's after hours."

At this point in the film we can see a basic pattern: Paul's kindness and conventionality are being reduced by irrational responses from those he meets. A good example of this occurs when he smokes some of Marcie's pot. He's been offered a joint earlier but refused. Now he needs to loosen up, if he can. But when he takes a few puffs, he suddenly "turns," accusing Marcie of giving him shit to smoke ("This isn't really pot"). His sudden hostility takes the viewer by surprise. Is this the real Paul, hidden from us and from himself by his good manners? He insists that Marcie get him one of the plaster bagel and cream cheese paperweights that Kiki makes, saying, "Right now there are important papers flying all around my apartment because I don't have anything to hold them down with." When Marcie goes to get the bagel, he leaves. It's as if he uses her momentary absence to escape. He is unable to leave in her presence. His passive-aggressive response to Marcie is intensified because he's also "flipping out." He can't get angry directly to Marcie about the games she's playing with him. Instead, he uses the pot and the bagel.

The increasingly bizarre nature of Paul's behavior with Marcie is seen at the very end of the Marcie segment of the film. Returning to her bedroom after another frustrated effort to get money to return home, he gives a long apologetic speech to Marcie, who is resting on the bed. Finally he discovers that she is dead, or at least comatose from an overdose of sleeping pills. Paul sits by her body and hesitantly, slowly removes the blanket from her leg, eventually exposing a tattoo on her upper thigh. Is he checking to verify the glimpse he had earlier? It's an odd time to do it. He then slowly and lingeringly removes the blanket from Marcie's shoulders, completely exposing her nearly naked body (she's wearing only a very brief string panty). The camera movement here is slow and sensual, following the blanket as it is withdrawn from her body. It's like Roger Vadim's shot of the naked Brigitte Bardot in *And God Created Woman*, full of voyeuristic languor. After the initial shock at discovering that Marcie is dead, Paul doesn't seem upset at all. Instead, he avails himself of Marcie's passive state to have a good look. The shots of Marcie's body aren't from his point of view. They enlist the viewer in the act of visual possession. There's a necrophilic note here which doesn't seem like Paul at all. There is the possibility, however, that Paul is looking for burn scars on Marcie's body. The script is at its most allusive state here. Earlier, while Paul was rubbing Kiki's shoulders, he begins a story of how, as a child, he spent a night in a hospital burn ward, though he wasn't burned. The nurse told him to keep his eyes closed, but he opened them once and saw . . . . Paul's narration stops there. Presumably he saw some horrible disfigurement at an impressionable age. This childhood trauma is beginning to well up as Paul experiences greater displacement into the irrational world of Soho. While Marcie is out of the room, he discovers some burn ointment prescribed for her and a book with pictures of badly burned people to which he reacts with shock and disgust (Scorsese gives a few fast frames of burned flesh). The exposure of dead Marcie's nudity to Paul's gaze, however ambiguous, has a definite sexual dimension. But Paul would have difficulty admitting to it. He doesn't seem aware, when Kiki's statue and TV are taken, that she hasn't been tied up by the robbers but by leather-clad Horst, whose elaborate knot tying suggests that he and Kiki have been enjoying her bondage—even though he is given a clue earlier when Kiki tells him that if he rubs her until it hurts "you'd be on the right track." He remains a naïf in a world where others accept deviant behavior with cool detachment.

Paul's next connection is with Julie (Teri Garr), a waitress at a local bar. Dressed in yellow, with a sunny, upbeat manner, Julie has a beehive hairdo and likes to sing pop songs from the '50s. She brings Paul out of the rain into her apartment. Her arrangement of rat traps around her carefully made bed looks almost like a piece of installation art. She's square and strange at the same time. She's very needy and wants Paul to stay, and he tries to avoid hurting her feelings though he is dying to get away and go home. Finally he loses control, as in the pot scene with Marcie, and slaps one of Kiki's bagels out of Julie's hand as she offers it (everyone is connected in this neighborhood drama). Later we see her posting notices claiming that Paul is the burglar who's been ripping off the neighborhood.

The Gail episode repeats the pattern we've seen in Julie. She's very kind and helpful at first, taking Paul in after she injures him with a taxi door. But she prevents him from making a phone call and her helpfulness turns aggressive and domineering. He tries to tell her how guilty he feels about Marcie's death, but she tells him to come off it. She takes leadership of the crowd pursuing Paul as a burglar after she sees Julie's notice. Paul flees from her and climbs up a fire escape where he witnesses a woman empty a revolver into a man in a nearby apartment. His condition at this point is revealed by his comment "I'm probably to blame for that."

The literary source of Paul's drama of increasing guilt is probably the writings of Franz Kafka. We're given a clear indication of this when Paul attempts to get by the doorkeeper at Club Berlin. The burly doorkeeper accepts money from Paul so that "you don't feel you've left anything untried." This brief sequence is a parody and homage to Kafka's "Before the Law," in which a man from the country tries to get past the doorkeeper at the outer gate of the law courts, where he hopes to be found not guilty.

The Soho world is equally without the possibility of release from guilt. The closest Paul comes to absolution—and it's not close at all—is in his frequent visits to the bathroom where he washes his face and tries to compose himself though in one bathroom there's an ominous graffito depicting a sharp-toothed shark or snake devouring a man's penis. Paul is caught in a labyrinth. When he does get past the doorkeeper, later on, he's engulfed in a madhouse maelstrom of rock dancers and is nearly given a Mohawk haircut. He can spot Kiki and Horst but can't get to them to borrow money for a taxi home. Scorsese is manning the spotlight from the rafters.

Paul's final two potential rescuers seem similarly impassive. The first is a gay man who assumes that Paul is making a sexual proposition. Paul has just thrown himself on his knees in the street ("What do you want from me?" "What have I done?") before he meets him. He is nearly incoherent and totally unaware that the man isn't interested in the story of his night's difficulties, which he gives him at length. A phone call to the police is regarded as a nut call, and they hang up.

June is the central character in the final segment of the film. She's the only customer in the Club Berlin, a place Paul flees to for safety from the pursuing crowd (a strange choice after his initial experience there). Her muteness and friendliness seem promising but she, too, turns odd ("What are you doing? You dance with me, are nice with me. Why are you doing this?"). In her studio she holds Paul in her arms, comforting him; then when the crowd threatens to enter, she encases him in a papier-mâché sculpture from which she won't release him. Paul has become the angst-filled sculpture he helped Kiki make. June's entrapment of Paul is the culmination of Julie's and Gail's unwillingness to let Paul leave. She helps him, but imprisons him. Only the robbers "free" him at the front door of his workplace. The final sequence shows the camera moving fluidly and briskly around the office as the day begins. Seated at his desk, still in a dusty daze, Paul is welcomed by his computer with a "Good morning, Paul." We aren't given any signals whether Paul is happy to be back; we can only assume he is. The nightmare is over. The (boring) world of normality has returned. In this sense, the Soho world is presented almost entirely as a comic freak show. The papier-mâché sculpture, the bagel paperweights, and the conceptual art performance (which doesn't occur) seem to be cheerfully spoofed. Only two Soho characters seem relatively rational. Kiki is low-keyed and self-accepting, even in her taste for bondage. Tom, the bartender, Marcie's husband, really tries to help Paul. True, his key chain is decorated by a skull in a top hat, an image repeated in the tattoo on Marcie's thigh. The Soho crowd is weirder than Paul, even in his repressed state. They may act out their fantasies or their neuroses, whereas Paul is hardly capable; but their acting out is both comic and threatening. Paul won't be getting a tattoo any time soon, and the film welcomes it.

In visual terms, *After Hours* is one of Scorsese's least interesting films. The script is too fast-paced to permit silent passages in which the camera and soundtrack do the work. The strategy is to keep Paul moving quickly from one disorienting incident to another in a light and amusing fashion. This works well; the film is witty and entertaining. The chief charge against the visuals is that they don't change into more and more distorted images as Paul's guilt and paranoia grow. The model here is Welles' film adaptation of Kafka's *The Trial*, a film which Scorsese alludes to in the doorkeeper sequence ("Before the Law" is part of the Kafka novel, and Welles uses it as a prologue to his film). Welles' use of the abandoned D'Orsay train station in Paris—its upper catwalks and odd nooks and crannies, its voluminous cathedral-like lower spaces and huge clock—his expressionist lighting and use of lens distortion give vivid display to K's (Anthony Perkins) angst. *After Hours* uses Kafka but doesn't enter visually into his irrational, dream-like world. There are some fine signature shots of the oily, rain-slick streets, steam rising from the grates (as in *Taxi Driver*), but this is a kind of poetic realism rather than the nightmare hallucination of *The Trial* or Polanski's *The Tenant. After Hours* reveals Scorsese as essentially a realist.

More disturbing and damaging is the film's portrayal of women. As agents of Paul's disorientation, Marcie, Julie, Gail, and June are uniformly hurtful. Each promises comfort and each turns destructive. They are sirens luring Paul to his death. By comparison Tom, the bartender, and the gay man who listens to Paul's story seem beneficent. Men don't promise one thing and provide another. Women, on the other hand . . . well, they pull out a gun and empty it into you.

It's possible to argue that Scorsese's misogyny isn't there at all, that the women's behavior is not bizarre or threatening in itself but only as perceived by Paul's increasingly stressed consciousness. The script by Minion aims at this but the visuals, again, don't enforce the idea of subjective distortion. The Julie segment is a good example. Except for the rat traps surrounding the bed her apartment seems retro and square like her (we see a rat caught while Paul is there). Her abrupt shift from cheerful to angry isn't presented as a shift within Paul but rather as a hurt reaction to a dismissive "gee whiz" he utters. Her neediness ("You're not going to leave me now, are you?") is prompted by her worry that her anger will drive him away. Her gift of the bagel which provokes his anger is visually presented as a realistic gesture, not as a fantasy on Paul's part in which Julie is connected to Kiki and Marcie—different people but essentially one threatening woman. Similarly, Gail, the ice-cream vendor, comes across as hostile in herself rather than as an extension of Paul's imagination. Paul turns to each of the women except Kiki seeking comfort and finds himself wounded.

Scorsese's visual strategy in *After Hours* was to portray the irrational in realistic terms. A few shots like the threatening wad of keys that Kiki throws down to him, the shifting light in the hallway near Marcie's room where he hears voices, and the bar-like shadows of the stair rail against the wall in Tom's apartment have the distortion which accentuates Paul's inner state but there aren't many of these and they don't intensify. The posse of neighbors in the street looking for Paul is a real posse; there are real robbers at work; there really is the graffito in the bathroom. It's odd that Scorsese didn't use more of the expressionist visuals we've seen in earlier films.

Chapter 9

AN HOMAGE AND
A CAREER CHOICE

THE COLOR OF MONEY, 1986

The opportunity to make a sequel to Robert Rossen's *The Hustler* must have been appealing to Scorsese—both as a tribute to the fine older film and a chance, once again, for a big hit in the casting of Paul Newman as an older Eddie Felson, the pool player. But, while not a remake, a sequel inevitably compels comparison, and *The Color of Money* falls short. *The Hustler* (1961) is full of the atmosphere of seedy bars, pool halls, and flophouses, the marginal environment in which damaged creatures try to survive. The elemental savagery of its gritty interiors undoubtedly derives from the poverty and violence that Rossen experienced growing up in the Lower East Side of New York City in the '20s and '30s. The film also benefits from the brilliant casting of Newman as the young brash Eddie, Piper Laurie as his crippled companion, and George C. Scott as the shark-like manager who sees that behind Eddie's skill and flash there's the shadow of a born loser. The pool hall ambiance of Rossen's film is accurate for the '50s—a time before pool playing went upscale in the '80s and '90s with the near disappearance of the straight poolhall tables now attached to family entertainment centers, video games by the wall. Televised pool contests now have a sanitized feeling. There's more money in the game but less atmosphere, and the single shrunken table in a bar has wider pockets.

The script for *The Color of Money* by Richard Price, who was later to do the script *Life Lessons* for Scorsese, has a solid spine: the revival of skill and spirit in an older man under the pressures of the game. We've seen this idea so many times in film (*High Noon* is a good example) that any treatment runs the danger of mere formula. Price's script doesn't entirely skirt this problem for Scorsese, particularly in the latter half of the film where we see Eddie's comeback occurring in predictable but also confusing patterns. Newman's attractiveness (not the least, his physical attractiveness in which he's always perfectly dressed and groomed) makes the audience want to root for him. Tom Cruise as Vincent, playing the hotshot role Newman had in *The Hustler*, is so brash and self-congratulatory, with his hair rising up in a column from his head like a high school kid, that we want to see him taken down a peg or two. And who better to do it than Newman? When Eddie stops being Vincent's stake horse and teacher and becomes his opponent the formula is in play and the audience's energies are enlisted too easily for Eddie and against Vincent.

Vincent is a gifted pool player. He has "the eye, the stroke, and the flake" but he can't learn the "human moves" that Eddie tells him are at the center of the game. The script doesn't give him the complexity, the ability to grow in fits and starts, that would make Eddie's opposition to him more conflicted and interesting. He remains at the end the jerk he was in the beginning. We can't imagine that he'll ever become the strong, seasoned man Eddie has managed to become. Of course, life will test him as it did Eddie when he had his hands broken by the thugs he'd been hustling in *The Hustler*, but the film stops well short of that. It's really Eddie's story, not Vincent's.

Eddie's first appearance in the film establishes him as an authority figure. He's sitting at the bar with his girlfriend discoursing on the various properties of good whiskey, finger pointing up for emphasis. (There's a good deal of finger wagging in Newman's performance.) He's a successful liquor salesman now, totally out of the pool game. In his late fifties or early sixties, he speaks in a quiet raspy voice as she listens in rapt attention (has she heard any of this before?). He's beyond his prime but still in excellent shape and immaculately groomed. Those viewers who remember Newman's performance in *The Hustler* are likely to be aware at once of a pronounced transformation. *The Color of Money* nicely exploits the earlier film in the sense that it establishes an intriguing gap between the former broken Eddie and the new. How did he get this way? His comeback is a partial replication of this process but only partial. We never see or hear how he recovered in the intervening years. Instead we observe his attempts to help Vincent not make the mistakes he did. His interest in Vincent is both personal and impersonal: he sees his youthful self in Vincent, and his education of Vincent is a way to get back in the game but still keep it at a distance. He thinks that his stake horse role is just about making money but discovers his old fire in the process.

Vincent's inability to learn from Eddie is due to youthful exuberance and arrogance. He can't control his competitive energy. The first lesson Eddie tries to teach him is how to dump to a mediocre player in order to set up a big money match but Vincent can't hold back. In Chalkie's pool hall he beats the best player in the house, a tall, powerful black man in a big hat, and loses the chance to play a rich man who'll bet as much as $5,000 on a game. It's a telling sequence with one glaring fault: the audience's applause as Vincent dances and preens around the table. It's hard to imagine any knowledgeable group of pool spectators celebrating such arrogant behavior, no matter how good the shooter. In this sense Cruise's performance is a narcissistic inflation of Newman's earlier role, appropriate to our age.

When Vincent does follow Eddie's instructions to dump, it's under the wrong conditions. He's playing an old man with a hole in his throat and some sort of voice box and he can't take his money. Eddie's behavior here is strange: he instructs Vincent to dump "like a professional" (not like a soft-hearted kid) and then he arranges for them to skip out without paying the old man. This involves having Vincent's girlfriend Carmen wait outside the hall in the car while Eddie stages a rescue of Vincent from a dozen angry players by posing as his father who's outraged that his son has sneaked out to play pool. In the car Eddie says, "I saved your ass," but in fact he set up the attack by disappearing when the money was to be paid. Vincent has a pronounced bruise on his right cheek and temple and blood running from one side of his mouth. He has come close to being seriously injured. What lesson is Eddie teaching? To run out on a paltry

$90 debt? He tells Vincent, "You never ease off when money is involved," but his action is at odds with this message. The logic of the script here is scrambled. We're supposed to see Eddie as a wise instructor but he comes over as a devious and even sanctimonious guy (the finger wagging) who's unaware that as a stern "father" he wants his son punished. Remembering that young Eddie was seriously injured by pool hall thugs makes this episode all the more puzzling. Is he really trying to risk subjecting Vincent to the kind of injuries from which he had to recover? Vincent isn't going to make him any money in the hospital.

A key sequence midway in the film involves Eddie's frustration at Vincent's inability to learn from him (he's just beaten the big black guy he should have lost to). Eddie is disappointed and furious but he unaccountably opens up to Vincent as they sit in his car: "You've got me talking to myself. . . . Twenty-five years ago I had the screws put on me and it was over for me before it really got started. . . . I can always go back to whiskey but it's tired. You've made me hungry again. . . . You've bled it back into me." This monologue is useful to our understanding that Eddie wants Vincent to finish what he was unable to, that Vincent's success means much more than money to Eddie. But it's a long speech, full of declamation when few words, or none, would seem more appropriate to Eddie's feeling that he's wasting his breath. Yet it's from this point on that Vincent begins to follow Eddie's instructions and hustle effectively, culminating in his dumping to Grady Seasons, the best money player in the game.

Once Vincent's progress is under way, Eddie seems to back away as mentor. Vincent's improvement has provoked him to try a comeback. He doesn't need Vincent to complete his career for him. His loss to another hustler (Forest Whitaker in a brilliant cámeo) as Vincent and Carmen watch is so humiliating that he sends them on alone to the big tournament in Atlantic City, while he puts himself through rigorous training which culminates in his victory over Vincent in the tournament. Vincent's reaction to this defeat is full of bitterness. He shakes Eddie's outstretched hand without looking at him, doesn't acknowledge Eddie's comment that he shot a great game, and stalks off. Eddie's euphoria is blasted when, moments later a cheerful Vincent appears and gives him money for his cut, saying he placed a side bet on him and dumped to him. Vincent explains all this at length to Eddie's girlfriend, still unable to look at Eddie. He vivaciously describes the key moment when he seemed to choke on a fairly easy side pocket shot and says he calibrated the miss perfectly. Carmen seems to go along with his story. This is the most interesting moment in the film. He's probably telling the truth and his bitterness at the end of the game was just acting. It's also possible though far less likely that he's lying to save face. In any case, he's become a subtle student of "human moves" almost overnight, for he has knocked the pins out from Eddie in a diabolically clever way. He's no longer the sweet guy Carmen describes to Eddie earlier in the film who can't take the old player's money. He's mad at Eddie for abandoning him a few weeks before the tournament and wants revenge. Eddie's work at transforming him has paid off in the searing experience of Vincent's "deception." He's momentarily the naïve Mark and Vincent the pro. The role reversal which is the fulcrum of Price's script is complete. We're supposed to have an uneasy and generally unfavorable feeling about Vincent at this point. At the very least, he certainly lacks Eddie's character, which is demonstrated when Eddie defaults his next match uncertain that he won fairly over Vincent. His challenge to Vincent for another game to settle the issue is curiously marked by pleadings: "How long do you want me to fry? . . . Want to play kick the dog for the rest of your life? . . . I don't have a leg to stand on but I'm asking you." A moment later, once Vincent agrees to play, Eddie is fully confident, telling him, "If I don't beat you now, I'll beat you in Houston." He has set Vincent up for the showdown. The final shot of the film shows a smiling Eddie. "I'm back," he says.

Lawrence Friedman's comment that "Eddie sets out to corrupt young Vincent" by teaching him how to hustle seems simplistic.[1] Hustling is not a corrupt or evil part of pool playing. Topflight players don't do it because they don't need to and they're known quantities; they give points or even games to their weaker opponents and then beat them. But for unknown players trying to perfect their skills, the hustle is a useful, if risky, way to earn money. It's better than a second job. In Vincent's case learning how to hustle involves learning how to control his rampant competitiveness, to key down his emotional exuberance, to ground himself. It's a way of becoming a stronger player. It's a way of teaching himself what losing feels like and of putting him in touch with himself. This isn't to say that hustling isn't shady as are many aspects of gambling. Eddie's comeback is partially rendered in religious terms. It's a spiritual rebirth in the sense that he's transformed himself from the cheap hustler of the earlier film to a man of character and grace. Scorsese uses such touches as organ music when Eddie enters the vast temple-like space where the tournament will take place. Again, we don't see the agony in the wilderness that must have occurred in the gap between the two films. This transformation was dramatized so well in *Raging Bull* that Newman chose Scorsese to direct

The Color of Money. By comparison, the religious dimension seems almost perfunctory in the latter film and has caused some critics to call it the most manufactured and least personal of Scorsese's films. However, like Ellen Burstyn's choice of Scorsese for *Alice Doesn't Live Here Anymore*, Newman's choice allowed him to make a commercially viable product and position himself within a skeptical industry so that he could eventually make *The Last Temptation of Christ*. In each case a deeply personal utterance (*Mean Streets, Raging Bull*) prompted a major actor to select him as director.

In visual terms a film about pool playing is a challenge. The visual space in which the game is played is rigidly confined to the table itself or to the hall. With his interest in filming action sequences, Scorsese was impressed by Rossen's work in *The Hustler*. Scorsese's own tactic is characterized by a nondramatic approach to individual games just as his extensive use of music avoids dramatic manipulation. He doesn't show the ebb and flow of a match and build up to key moments in which a ball is sunk or missed. He covers many more games than Rossen and doesn't have time to linger as Rossen does in his demonstration of young Eddie's penchant for losing big matches, for instance in the early match with Minnesota Fats (Jackie Gleason). He often keeps the camera moving around and slightly above the table as a player sets up his shot, thus giving us a good feeling for the player's three dimensional awareness of how one shot is linked to the next. Or he puts the camera on the table and shows a ball coming directly at us, then quickly away and toward the pocket. There are relatively few of the standard TV overhead shots. The attempt, as with *Raging Bull* and *Life Lessons*, is to put us in the center of the action. Thus there are several shots of the balls exploding around the table on the break. Pool, however, is a game of careful geometry and control. It isn't like boxing or action painting. As a result Scorsese sometimes overdoes it, as when he has Eddie and Vincent slam their balls into the pockets in their tournament match, something no good pool player does. There are fine individual shots, however: the reflection of Eddie's face in the eight ball just before he defaults, the slow upward pan to Eddie's face as he lifts the racking frame from the balls just before he sets up to break and says, "I'm back."

Paul Newman's ability to extract an Academy Award performance from a flawed script helped make *The Color of Money* a success, though it wasn't the big hit Scorsese had hoped for. The authenticity of the pool sequences was helped by Scorsese's insistence that Newman and Cruise make almost all of the many difficult shots themselves. They were of course aided by master players who set up the shots and showed them how to execute. One of these players is Eddie's first opponent in the Atlantic City tournament. His querulous insistence "I didn't deserve that" when he loses is an inside joke. There's no cutting in the midst of a shot which would allow Scorsese to "cheat." A couple of exceptions occur on 9-ball breaks in which the 9 is sunk, and the game won in one shot—probably the most difficult shot in the game—and an incredible shot in which Vincent "cowboys" the cue ball over two blocking balls and sinks the object ball in the corner. As with boxing in *Raging Bull*, the subculture of pool playing is given documentary-like attention. The best pros and also hangers-on form a backdrop to Eddie's and Vincent's foreground action. The character who plays Grady Seasons is clearly a professional player. His fluid, calm, delicate execution of shots suggests that Newman and Cruise are well-trained actors. Finally, like *Raging Bull*, *The Color of Money* isn't about pool but about the struggle for inner strength and self-knowledge. Eddie's demonstration that he has it and Vincent's that he may never get it are the two strong elements that drive the film.

Note

1. Lawrence Friedman, *The Cinema of Martin Scorsese* (New York: Continuum Publishing Co., 1998), 148.

Chapter 10

THE AGONY ON THE HILL

THE LAST TEMPTATION OF CHRIST, 1988

Scorsese's adaptation of Kazantzakis' novel, *The Last Temptation of Christ*, is a passionate, intensely felt, dramatic, and long (164 minutes) interpretation of Christ's sacrifice. The film is true to the ideology and spirit of the novel. It contains an interesting combination of the ideological and the visionary. It had long been a project Scorsese wanted to do and, after many reversals, when he finally got the money together, the producers remained nervous both about its cost and about controversial public reception. Scorsese addressed the cost issue by shooting most of the exteriors in Morocco, but he couldn't control the controversy. Fundamentalist religious groups, mainly in the United States, first tried to buy the rights to the film to prevent any showing; and when this strategy failed, they raucously picketed showings at theaters all over the United States, attempting to intimidate audiences from attending and theater owners from continuing to show the film. Controversy attracted some people who might not normally have come, but it also put a huge dent in attendance. The film didn't have long runs, except in major cities like New York and Los Angeles, and it failed to make money. Provoking passionate reactions, the film was reviled as heresy and anti-Christian, as well as a cinematic masterpiece. It is neither.

The story of the making of *The Last Temptation of Christ* is a saga in itself, the best account of which is given by Scorsese himself.[1] In brief, the idea for the film began when Barbara Hershey and David Carradine gave him a copy of the novel after they'd finished shooting *Boxcar Bertha* in 1972. Paul Schrader produced a script which was rejected by United Artists but accepted by Paramount, which later backed out under pressure from the fundamentalists. The film had already been cast and the locations chosen by this time. The budget was $16 million, a large sum in 1983. Scorsese began revising the script with an eye to reducing cost. The initial year's delay was not a loss because "we learned how *not* to make the picture."[2] Efforts to find funding continued in France and elsewhere to no avail. Only Scorsese's decision to leave his agent of twenty years, Harry Ufland, and go with Michael Ovitz produced results. Ovitz convinced Universal Studios to back the film and shooting began in 1987.

Kazantzakis wished to rescue Christ from overspiritualization. His Jesus is a man of passionate body as well as spirit. He drinks wine, dances, and has had sexual relations with women. His discovery of God within himself and of his spiritual mission is a slow, confused, and tortuous process and occupies the bulk of the novel and the film. He may share the stridency but he lacks the perfect certitude of Pasolini's Christ in *The Gospel According to St. Matthew.* He also lacks the mystic calm suggested in Bresson's religious films *Au Hazard Balthazar* and *Mouchette.* As Scorsese puts it, "The human nature of Jesus was fighting Him all the way down the line, because it can't conceive of Him being 'God.'"[3]

The Last Temptation of Christ has a rich visual texture. Scorsese wisely chose to use Moroccan folk culture as well as the magnificent landscape of the area on the desert side of the Atlas mountains. As a result, we have sequences of great strangeness and beauty, like the wedding celebration at which Jesus dances and turns water into wine. The faces of the guests, their dress, the music and the instruments (especially the drums), the slaughtering of the sheep (mostly off-screen) are both exotic and somehow familiar. We're looking at old rituals which have been passed down (and some would say thinned out) to this day. The strongest element is the landscape, arid, burnt tan and gold by the sun—an ancient place where prophets and messiahs rise up from the barrenness. This harshness makes the presence of water as a revivifying element more meaningful, as in the sequence in which John the Baptist baptizes Jesus. The landscape also produces dreamlike images which, in their strangeness, suggest that Jesus experiences God's message like an hallucination. The white-draped mourners whom Jesus encounters before he meets the dying master of a monastery appear like rock outcroppings at first; their soft moans and grievings have a haunting effect. Scorsese was aiming at a trance-like effect in the visuals, which is produced not only by the desert environment in itself but by the effect of that environment and of God's growing presence within Jesus. A good example of this occurs in the ten-shot sequence when Jesus casts out the devils. In shot 1 he's walking with his disciples when, in long shot, the devils emerge writhing and screaming in slow motion from holes in the ground. In shots 3 to 7 we see fast close-ups of the devils' attack on Jesus, their bodies heavily caked with sores. He throws them off one by one, increasingly exhausted by the effort. Judas holds him up. In shot 10 the devil sequence merges with a sequence in which Jesus heals a blind man. At the end of his energy, the presence of God within him enables a miracle. These images are powerful in their irrationality and in their ability to evoke the displacement Jesus is experiencing.

Other episodes capture the visionary process which Jesus is experiencing. The funeral procession for the master of a monastery occurs in an obscuring sandstorm at dusk, the mourners and white-wrapped body dimly seem like apparitions. The raising of Lazarus has some of the same hallucinatory effect. The sequence's thirty-three shots begin with several heavily draped mourners crouched next to a sandstone cliff. They appear at first like rock outcroppings until we see them begin to move and we hear their soft mournful screeching. Jesus will, a few shots later, nearly become a part of the landscape himself as Lazarus' strong grip pulls him into the tomb. The disciples and other observers are appalled at Lazarus' stench but Jesus overcomes his initial repulsion. In shot 15 the camera pulls back from behind Jesus and the whole screen fills with the blackness of the tomb into which he's been gazing. In shots 31 through 33 Lazarus, half-dead, falls forward into an embrace of Jesus and Jesus experiences a moment of terror, crying out to God to help him. He can transcend Lazarus' smell but his human desire to cling to life produces a spasm of death fear.

The Lazarus episode is heavily dramatic. The episode of Jesus in the wilderness is less so, though it is full of visions. Sitting within a perfect circle which he has marked out in the earth, Jesus experiences a series of temptations. A black cobra appears and speaking in the voice of Mary Magdalene (Barbara Hershey) tells Jesus he's afraid of being alone and offers loving and sexual companionship. A lion appears and offers Jesus control of "any country you want." The voice is the worldly Judas' (Harvey Keitel). A pillar of fire appears and tells Jesus he can be God. The twenty-three shots in this sequence appear to have been shot at night using special lenses and film stock, and the dimness of the ambient light, as in the funeral procession, lends a spectral effect.

In terms of the verbal text, *Temptation* has a coherent but flawed structure. Paul Schrader, who also wrote the script for *Taxi Driver*, wanted to key down the Biblical language to more ordinary uses, just as Kazantzakis wanted to make Christ as much man as spirit. Sometimes the use of ordinary speech doesn't work very well, as when Jesus is first refused entrance to the wedding celebration and one of the disciples says, "these people are my guests," or when Jesus begins a parable: "I'm sorry. The easiest way to make myself clear." This is a minor quibble. On the whole, the script admirably accomplishes the translation of the novel's ideology. Scorsese quotes Kazantzakis in an epigraph to the film:

> The dual substance of Christ—the yearning so human, so superhuman, of man to attain God . . . has always been a deep inscrutable mystery to me. My principle anguish and source of all my joys and sorrows from my youth onward has been the incessant, merciless battle between the spirit and the flesh . . . and my soul is the arena where these two armies have clashed and met.

This dialectic involves a series of conversations, or confrontations, Jesus (Willem Dafoe) has with various characters. Judas is the most important character here, and he is elevated in importance far above his place in the Biblical story. He's a devil's advocate, constantly challenging Jesus, without being an agent of Satan. His six conversations with Jesus can be viewed as the armature of the film.

In their first exchange, Judas challenges Jesus for continuing to make crosses on which the Romans crucify rebellious citizens. He accuses Jesus of cowardice in doing the Romans' work. Jesus even helps put people on the crosses and measures the width of his arms on a crosspiece he's making. He's got a guilty obsession with crucifixion. Judas tries to shake him out of this, but Jesus is agonizingly possessed by spirits which may be God or the devil; he's not sure which. The third confrontation begins as a debate over whether the body or the soul is the foundation of belief but turns dangerous when Judas tells Jesus he's been ordered to kill him (he's actually pulled a knife on Jesus in the second episode). Jesus' manner disarms him and he ends up comforting Jesus by sleeping beside him during the night. This incident is the best early example of Jesus' power to convert, but it's an uneasy conversion on Judas' part. In number four Jesus explains to Judas why he must die willingly on the cross and that he'll come back to judge the living and the dead. As usual Judas plays the doubter, but Jesus calmly insists, "You have to believe me." This sequence is marked by a quiet power so different from the turbulence and emotional intensity of much of the film. Jesus has by this time achieved an inner strength that is both attractive to Judas and provokes his resentment. The fifth episode is essentially a repetition of four, but number six shows us Jesus as an old man on his deathbed visited by Judas and the other disciples, and it is Judas, true to form, who accuses Jesus of selling out in failing to go through with the crucifixion. Jesus, in turn, shows his greatest affection to Judas. It's as if he's always needed his opposite figure to keep him strong. It is Judas who points out to Jesus that the angel who convinces him to lead a normal life as a married man is an agent of Satan. Jesus doesn't seem aware of this. Only after Judas challenges him does Jesus crawl from his deathbed, seeking to submit to the crucifixion. True to the ideology of the novel, Jesus' power is the product of opposing forces. His faith isn't characterized by easy resolution but by constant struggle. The writings of the British poet and minister John Donne come to mind. Judas' point of opposition seems to fluctuate according to Jesus' growth. He's a negativist who needs Jesus as much as Jesus needs him.

The other figures who challenge Jesus are John the Baptist, Mary Magdalene, and Saul. Mary (Barbara Hershey) tells Jesus that he's just like the others in his sexual desires but can't admit it. Their exchange takes place at the end of a sequence that proved to be one of the flash points of controversy about the film—Mary's sexual servicing of several men. Actually, this sequence is one of the best in the film; it's not lurid or even very explicit. Mary has sex with the men behind a gauze curtain at one end of the room while the others, including Jesus, sit quietly, chatting or playing board games as they await their turn. There's no leering or dirty jokes or ribald excitement. A natural exchange is taking place. The camera sometimes notices Mary in the background. The calmness in the room is accentuated as the mellow light of late afternoon turns into evening. Jesus waits until he can speak with her. She's angry with him for abandoning her for God. The implication is that their prior relationship was a sexual one, that one reason Mary became a prostitute is because of her rejection by Jesus, and that Jesus feels guilty for what has happened to her. Her anger turns to love after he rescues her from a stone-throwing mob and she becomes one of his most devoted followers.

In the exchange with John the Baptist, John tells Jesus to abandon nonviolent means and take up the sword. His accusation puts Jesus once again to the test, for he moves back and forth between love and aggression throughout the film as he tries to find his way. Saul (Harry Dean Stanton) tells him the Jesus that people have invented in order to believe is much more important than the real Jesus. He asserts the power of myth over reality and leaves Jesus yearning to have carried out his crucifixion.

Scorsese's (and Kazantzakis') fondness for incidents of high drama gives the film a super-charged energy. Sometimes these incidents work well, as in the Golgotha sequence, but at other moments they don't. As Jesus stands before the tomb, Lazarus' arm pops up stiffly out of the darkness. It's a hokey incident. When Jesus converses with a young priest after the death of the master of the monastery, he tells the priest that "God wants to push me over," and the camera abruptly echoes his words by nearly toppling over into a nearby chasm—a minor but unnecessary excess. At the very end of the crucifixion, which ends the film, there are jagged abstract images as if the camera, or the projector, has broken down. This is almost a direct quote from Bergman's *Persona*; and though Scorsese means to suggest emotional overload and—as in *Persona*—to remind us that we're watching a film, it doesn't work very well.

The main problem in the film concerns the final angel episodes which are far too long. As Jesus struggles on the cross, a young girl appears, removes the nails from his hands and feet and informs him that God wants him to live a normal life. He returns home to Mary Magdalene, she nurses his wounds, they make love but she dies before she can bear his child. There is an unreality to her death, which is probably intentional, as is the artificial soft lighting and the setting of the house in which they live. The images are from a fairy tale. Jesus rages at her death and picks up an axe and storms out of the house. But the angel counsels him to find another woman, and he ends up living with two women who both bear him children. He's the head of a large family when he encounters Saul who tells him the real Jesus doesn't matter and he's an old man on his deathbed when the disciples come to say goodbye. All of this material takes about twenty-five minutes to present before we return to Jesus on the cross and the realization that he has been experiencing a prolonged fantasy in which his human desires assert themselves for the last time. The length of the angel section underlines his humanness, his bodyfulness, but it also breaks up the power of the crucifixion. True, it is placed at the end of the Golgotha section, but it could have been shortened by half and been more effective. We simply don't need to experience Jesus' fantasy life in such detail. The visual procedure in this section is the opposite of visionary. Its soft realism makes tepid Jesus' intense desire to remain human. His earlier experiences of God's calling are far more unsettling.

The high point of *Temptation* is the crucifixion itself. Jesus, who helped to crucify others in the beginning of the film, is now the crucified. The sequence begins with an overhead shot of Jesus carrying the crosspiece, then a slow-motion shot from eye level of Jesus surrounded by a mocking rabble. This shot is intensified by even greater slow motion in the next shot, in which we're brought closer to Jesus and the rabble seems to press nearer. It's a shot almost without depth in which his sorrowing form stands in the same plane as those who accompany him, like the great images of the crucifixion by Hieronymus Bosch. This shot is accompanied by a keening voice and the sound of an organ. In the right foreground a small, hooded, white-faced woman stands with no expression, unlike the others who are grinning and grimacing as in Bosch. The camera travels up Golgotha and we see various black-clad mourners, almost all women, who are outnumbered by the curious and the derisive ones. The pounding of the nails is done in several fast shots in which we see the hammer lifted, brought down, blood spurting, the nails piercing through the wood. This and other shots are repetitions and refinements of the crucifixion shots at the end of *Boxcar Bertha*, the film in which Scorsese rehearsed the ending of *Temptation*. An overhead shot shows Jesus and the cross lifted into position, the camera traveling upward as the cross rises. A storm begins to rage as the camera, shooting Jesus from the side, slowly tilts ninety degrees as he cries, "Why have you forsaken me?" The angel appears after the sound abruptly ceases. The soundtrack here is very close to the storm sounds of the final Robinson fight in *Raging Bull*. Jesus' acceptance of his role, after the angel episode, is equally powerful. Contorted on the cross, he raises his joyful face to utter, "It is accomplished." The effect of the angel section doesn't act to place him in a state of ambiguity; his final gesture is one of complete resolution.

This magnificent ending is accompanied by the screeching sound of mourners. The music throughout by Peter Gabriel is one of the film's triumphs. Using an eclectic mix of Egyptian, Moroccan, Brazilian, and electronic sounds, Gabriel fashioned a score that is at once primitive, universal, and sublime.

Notes

1. *Scorsese on Scorsese*, 116-145.
2. Ibid., 121.
3. Ibid., 124.

Chapter 11

THE ARTIST AS AGONIST

LIFE LESSONS
(from *New York Stories, 1990*)

Martin Scorsese's central characters are almost always obsessive-compulsive, driven men who seek their salvation through a process of violent self-expression and redemption.

In *Life Lessons*, Scorsese's only treatment of a visual artist, the painter Lionel Dobie is both representative of this basic pattern and anomalous to it. Like Travis Bickle in *Taxi Driver* and Jake LaMotta in *Raging Bull*, Dobie acts out his torments on his furiously painted canvases. Unlike them, he doesn't experience a breakthrough into spiritual awareness which releases him from his torment. He needs his torment to remain creative. Like Scorsese himself he reenacts in his work a basic pattern in a series of variations. The origin of the film is Dostoyevsky's *The Gambler*, in which the central character, a writer, slavishly pursues a younger woman who rejects him. Richard Price, the script writer, felt that the film's main character should be a painter—that a writer would be too static. The young woman in the film is also a painter, though less gifted. The film examines an idea that appeared in *New York, New York*: a conflicted relationship between artists/performers in which one (always a man) is considerably more talented than the other.

Life Lessons is the first film in a trilogy of short films by Francis Ford Coppola, Woody Allen, and Scorsese known as *New York Stories*. It's by far the best of the three. The Coppola segment *Life Without Zoe* is an expensively produced embarrassment, and the Allen *Oedipus Wrecks* is an amusing series of jokes about mother domination. If Scorsese worried about appearing in close comparison with two of North America's best directors, he needn't have. *Life Lessons* has the freshness and force of his best work. It is, in my opinion, one of his three or four best films (along with *Raging Bull, Taxi Driver* and *The King of Comedy*).

Two things, besides Scorsese's direction, help achieve the excellence of the film: a fine, strong script by Price and a superb acting job by Nick Nolte as Lionel Dobie. When we first encounter the famous New York painter Dobie, he's in a state of anxiety about an upcoming show, three weeks away, for which he's done very little work. The opening shots suggest his agitation: close-ups of his pacing feet, of a lit cigarette in his fist, of a dirty brandy glass from which he takes a sip. It should be noted here that Scorsese begins immediately with these energetic tight shots, holding off the establishing shot of Dobie's studio. Much of the film's rhythm comes from Dobie's galvanic, gestural painting style (three sequences in particular which show him attacking the canvas with spontaneous strokes of the brush, using a trash can lid as his palette). Scorsese's abrupt camera work catches exactly the frenzy and torment and pleasure of Dobie's way of working. Like Scorsese himself, he's getting the angst out in a creative way. You could say that Dobie is a painterly version of Scorsese as a filmmaker, or that Scorsese would paint like Dobie if he were a painter. He has to paint; it's not a choice. His art is sacred to him; it provides a form of salvation in a bad life. He paints from the guts, searching for authenticity in spontaneity. Most of all, as *Life Lessons* makes clear, Dobie paints from the torment of sexual rejection.

His assistant, Paulette (Rosanna Arquette), is fed up with him, and has been planning to leave. Yet Dobie drives to the airport to pick her up from a trip. He needs her around, or rather he needs her rejection at close hand to kick him into high intensity production. The stenciled name on his truck is "Russian Roulette Inc." Every new painting is like a life-risking effort. If he weren't a painter he might well be a criminal.

In Paulette's room, he watches avidly as she folds her panties into her suitcase. Later that evening, he comes into her room from his painting, ostensibly to ask if the music is too loud. He gazes at her naked foot (an iris shot which then becomes a close-up). His foot obsession expresses his desire for rejection: he wants to kiss her foot, to abase himself before her. The large number of iris shots scattered throughout the film emphasize Dobie's selective eye. He also uses his considerable charm and persuasiveness to convince Paulette to stay ("You work for the lion, in the heart of the heart, you get life lessons which are priceless"). She agrees to stay as long as they don't have sex any more. Dobie returns to work with fresh vigor, looking away from the canvas from time to time at Paulette's window. When she asks him if he loves her and what would he do if she left, he crouches on her bed and says enthusiastically, "I'd go up on the roof and howl like a gut-shot dog." The next sequence shows him painting ferociously, as he does later when Paulette is in her room with Toro, a new lover. The best visual detail in the furious painting sequences is a small tormented face peering out of the thick impasto—Dobie's own, of course.

What Dobie wants from Paulette is fairly clear. What she wants is validation from him; she wants him to tell her that she's got basic talent and should go on painting. In a sense, she withholds sex from him because he withholds the validation, which she regards as a cruel manipulation on his part. But he feels he can't give her the definitive statement she seeks, nor can anyone. She has to find out for herself and if she stops painting then she wasn't a real artist anyway. This exchange occurs a bit past the middle of the film and after it Dobie stomps off muttering the phrases he's just used to Paulette in a savagely self-critical way. He distrusts his own words more than the images he creates. And yet we should note how very good with words he is—how subtle in his manipulations. In part this is due to the fact that Richard Price is a stronger wordman than the painter who executed the canvases for the film is as a creator of visual images. At the airport, in her room, in the studio, he reasons with Paulette, slowly bending her to his needs. Only at the cocktail party does he fail to use words successfully, and it's a very revealing moment. Having dragged her off to the bathroom in a rage at Toro's advances, he tells her that everyone is laughing at her. She says she thought they were laughing at her work and his reply is that their laughter at her behavior with Toro is "kinda worse, don't you think?" That's about how clearly he sees the importance of her painting to her.

Life Lessons is about Lionel Dobie but it's also about the creation of a single painting. We see the nearly blank canvas (a very large one, about an 8x20 foot rectangle) at the beginning of the film. And we see the finished painting hanging behind the bar at Dobie's opening, in the final sequence. In between we see the work evolve from a series of tentative black squiggles and lines on the white canvas to a chaotic mishmash of frenzied strokes to the shaping armature of a series of arches like a bridge leading into nowhere. The arches are probably derived from the arched windows on one side of the studio. In any case it's a pleasure to watch the work develop and to feel the energy and gusto that goes into it. The painting sequences put us up close to the canvas and move our eye rapidly from the trash-can palette to the actual strokes of the brush. It's as if we're doing the painting ourselves. Like the boxing sequences in *Raging Bull* Scorsese puts us in the middle of the action. It's all done with such passion that it seems temporizing to ask how good the painting really is, but we have to. After all, Lionel Dobie is a world-famous painter. Like the later Pollock of the meshed dribbles, whom he mentions, his work rests a good deal on chance. Some of the works we glimpse in the final show are downright bad. The big painting we've been following isn't really very good, but that's always the case with films about contemporary painters, like *The Horse's Mouth*, in which the director has to find an artist to do the painting while the camera rolls. De Kooning wasn't available; the enmeshed, tormented Pollock dead.

The important thing is that we get caught up in Dobie's action-oriented style of painting. Not for him the carefully controlled, meditative style of a Diebenkorn, Judd, or Marden. A film about a painter in this style wouldn't interest Scorsese, who may be concerned with salvation but not with transcendence or contemplative calmness. Whether Dobie's painting is really good is, in the final analysis, a marginal question. The film makes us believe it's really good by establishing a riveting dramatic context within which we see the work grow in strength.

One of the ways Scorsese convinces us that Dobie is really good is through the conventional means of reaction shots. We see Dobie lionized by art dealers, collectors, other painters at his opening and at a black tie dinner for a long-time art patron. The most extensive of these sequences involves Paulette's attempt to get Dobie's attention while he's at work.

She comes into his working space in an angry mood; she needs an immediate response from Dobie but he's totally absorbed in the painting (we're given fast cutting in extreme close-up of the paint going onto the canvas and shots of Dobie's intense face, along with the galvanic rhythms of the rock music "Like a Rolling Stone"). Gradually, Paulette's expression changes from anger to admiring wonder at Dobie's confident, swashbuckling painting style. He's her (and our) ideal of what a great abstract expressionist painter should be. The rock music which accompanies most of Dobie's work is a perfect choice by Scorsese to emphasize the slashing galvanic energy with which he lays down the paint.

Another visual way in which Scorsese presents Dobie is through his handling of the studio's space. Like many New York studios, Dobie's is essentially one large room with the arched windows along one side (like most abstract expressionists Dobie isn't interested in natural light; he works mainly at night). One oddity is the placement of Paulette's room; it's reached by a stairway and projects out into the studio's upper space. Its "windows" have been crudely hammered open through the brick walls and give on to the studio space. As he works below, Dobie is constantly aware of the desirable Paulette lounging around her bed in dishabille, on the phone to friends and admirers. As he gazes intently up at his large canvas, Dobie has only to move his eyes slightly to the right to see Paulette's window. Scorsese often has his camera moving in an arc from behind Dobie (thus also showing the canvas) to a side shot in which we see the window. The relationship between these two apertures, painting and window, is most clearly seen in a fine six-shot sequence late in the film. Dobie has returned alone from the birthday party, thrown off his tux coat and shirt, and begun to paint; Paulette is up in her room with the young artist Toro whom she met at the party. The sequence begins with a three-part shot which is accompanied by eloquent music by Puccini which Dobie has turned on, replacing his usual rock music. In the first part of the shot we see Dobie slumped in his chair, his eyes are nearly closed, the warm flesh tones of his upper body contrasting with the darkness of his surroundings. As the opera singer reaches a poignant phrase Dobie rises and approaches the camera which backs off, keeping him at middle distance. He's looking up in an emotional way (at the painting or the window?). In the third part of the shot Dobie moves into a close-up as the aria reaches its emotional climax. We can see the anguish in his eyes behind his paint-flecked glasses. The choreography of this shot according to the emotional phrasing of the aria is particularly effective. The aria "Nessum Dorma" (no one sleeps) from Puccini's *Turandot* evokes

Dobie's restless style; we know where Paulette sleeps, but we never see Dobie at rest or know if he even has a bed. The second shot makes clear where he's looking; it's a medium long shot of the studio with Dobie gazing up at the window. The third shot gives us a slow pan of the painting and in the fourth Toro appears (it's now morning) and asks Dobie for a cup of coffee as the music fades out. Shot 5 begins with Toro startled at a loud cry of triumph from the opera singer; as he quickly turns his head, he sees (shot 6) Dobie in his bathrobe, feverishly at work on the painting. Dobie turns away from the canvas and looks at Toro, breaking slowly into a smile of deep pleasure. He's recovered from his anguish, or rather put it to use in the only way he knows will really work. This brief sequence is a kind of miniature of the entire film. As Dobie says, "I indulge in love and indulge in making my stuff and they feed off each other."

In the final sequence, Dobie meets another nubile young woman at his opening and makes her the same offer he's made to Paulette, who has taken off: free room and board and "life lessons." The iris shots which both close and open the film, and which evoke the painter's (or filmmaker's) eye, also suggest an iron circularity to Dobie's own behavior. He can't or won't change his behavior. The life lessons he offers are for his women, not for him. He may see himself as a teacher, but he's not a learner. As his dealer says to him early in the film when he's in a state of anxiety about his coming opening, "Get to know yourself a little better; you go through this every time." Dobie is a good example in painting of what the psychologists call the compulsion to repeat. Do his paintings ever change and deepen? His behavior in this brief fragment from his life suggests they do not. His art is not the product of a striving for self-knowledge, sanity, and calmness. He's not after transcendence and removal from torment and anxiety, which he and Scorsese would regard as a turning away from life. He's also not after redemption, like other Scorsese heroes. He may be in a kind of "hell" with Paulette but it's a creative hell which produces paintings, some of which look like volcanic eruptions. His painting is sacred, as he tells Paulette, but he's not on a religious quest. He wants to remain where he is, and were he asked he'd undoubtedly have very eloquent words to describe why. All in all, *Life Lessons* remains a wonderful evocation of one kind of modern painting.

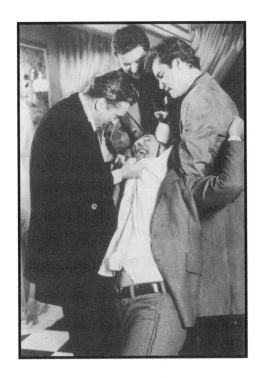

Chapter 12

THE REAL CREW

GOODFELLAS, 1991

Scorsese's film *Goodfellas* is based on the book *Wiseguy* by Nicholas
Pileggi, with whom he wrote the script. Like the book, the film presents
the mob as it really is, not as a romanticized, close-knit family. Scorsese's
documentary impulse is best seen in the film. *Goodfellas* can be regarded
as Scorsese's reply to the high style, grand opera treatment of Coppola in
The Godfather, just as Pileggi's book is a reply to Mario Puzo's novel.

The film demonstrates Scorsese's realism, though it is not without a romanticized, fairy-tale dimension. Pileggi's realism in the book is constant; there aren't any excursions into fantasy and surrealism as in the brutal stomping of the mobster Billy Batts in the movie—blood spurting up onto the killers from Batts' body on the barroom floor, or the hellishly lit sequence when Batts' deliquescent body has to be dug up. Pileggi's matter-of-factness has few moments of comic distortion, while Scorsese's film is often hilarious in its presentation of the excesses of mob life. *Goodfellas* is, at least in its first half, a very funny film (Tommy would ask with barely disguised threat a "funny how?" But he is safely confined to the screen). Its early humor is partly connected to the excitement and pleasure Henry Hill is experiencing in the mob. As he witnesses more and more cruelty, and comes under threat himself, this playful humor dissolves into blackness and savagery.

The film is a fast-paced narrative of Henry's life in the mob, from his youth as a "gofer" and numbers runner to his activities as a drug dealer and eventual escape into the federal witness protection program. The opening sequence, a kind of brief prologue before the credits, establishes Henry's ambivalent position quickly. Henry (Ray Liotta) is driving at night into the countryside with his fellow mobsters, Jimmie (Robert De Niro) and Tommy (Joe Pesci), to dispose of the body of Batts whom Tommy and Jimmie have just killed in a bar fight argument. When the body starts banging around in the trunk, they stop and stab and shoot the near-dead corpse as Henry watches in shock, just as he watched the attack in the bar. Immediately after this brief sequence Henry, thinking of his youth, tells us "as far back as I can remember I always wanted to be a gangster." Such ironic juxtaposition is a basic strategy in the film. The large knife Tommy uses in the stabbing is his mother's kitchen implement, and she insists the three sit down to a good home-cooked meal as the camera wanders past the cheerful, nervous eaters to the car where the corpse twitches and bangs. Scenes of family celebration are followed by brutal violence in truck hijackings, debt collection; a night out with his mistress, Janet, at the Copacabana is followed the next day by a large family gathering at his boss Paulie's. In one of the best lengthy sequences, Henry juggles cooking a special dinner for his family and crippled brother with gun dealing and preparation (and heavy use with his mistress, Sandy) of cocaine for a shipment. In this sequence the camera is constantly glancing up, like Henry, at a helicopter which seems to be pursuing him. There's a fast-paced, ragged rhythm to the cutting between his various activities. The feeling of paranoia, of being strung out, is palpable. It's a jangled, fragmented existence which Henry describes as if it were normal. The irony in *Goodfellas* is without romantic nostalgia, moral posturing, or judgmentalism. It's mob life from the inside.

The images in the film are organized largely according to the voice-over narration, with a few longer sequences fully dramatized. Since Henry is giving us a comprehensive summary of his life (and isn't a novelist who wants to elaborate), the pace of the images is brisk and elliptical, brief glimpses into long passages of time. This is especially true of the later portions of the film when Henry is speeding on coke and full of anxiety and paranoia (the dinner, gun, and coke-dealing sequence mentioned earlier is the best example). In this sense, Scorsese, who has had his problems with cocaine in the distant past and who has a speedy rhythm anyway, is one of our best artists to express in film the feeling of drugs (another is Gus Van Sant).

Scorsese and Pileggi are interested in the mundane culture of the mob more than in its spectacular and violent activities. Henry and his wife, Karen (Lorraine Bracco), give two different perspectives into that culture; she's an outsider from a "respectable" middle-class Jewish family. In a middle section of the film devoted mainly to her narration, we see her awareness of the strangeness of going out with Henry, who is only twenty-one, to a ring-side table at the Copacabana and having everyone fawn over them (the long, steadycam shot of their entry through the basement and the kitchen, which received so much attention, has a documentary feeling to it). One part of her wants to normalize her experience, as when she describes Henry and his friends as "blue-collar guys" who simply "cut a few corners." Another part is both shocked and pleased when she receives cash in envelopes from the guests at her wedding, many of whom, she observes, are called Peter or Paul and who are all married to women called Marie. She's a rebel from her own family's domestic quietude; she doesn't back away when Henry gives her a gun to hide for him. The other part of her finds mob culture weird. This is best illustrated in a hilarious sequence when one of the wives gives a hostess party where the ladies try different cosmetics. These women talk as tough as their men and discuss extreme violence without distress. They have wild bouffant hairdos and try out blue face cream. This is the way Karen puts it: "They had bad skin and wore too much makeup. They looked beat up and the stuff they wore was thrown together and cheap—a lot of pantsuits and double knits. They talked about how rotten their kids were and about how they beat them with broom handles and still these kids didn't pay any attention." This loud, raucous, coarse, comic sequence isn't satirical or ironic; it's the way things are. Karen never becomes like these women; she does join Henry in his cocaine addiction, however, and somehow manages to keep the family together while Henry is in jail. Her comment about cutting a few corners is immediately followed by a violent hijack scene in which a terrified driver is roughed up and Tommy and Henry drive off with his load, Tommy shooting into the sky through a paper bag he's used to conceal his weapon. "I got to admire my husband for having the enterprise to go out and get us the little extras," she says and we see Henry's closet with fifty suits and hers with even more dresses. In the latter half of the film, as things darken, she's moved beyond normality into nearly committing violence herself as she pulls a gun on Henry (we see close-ups of the weapon) and accuses him of going with whores. When the police raid their house she stuffs a gun down the front of her brief panties.

Henry's perspective as an insider is more complex. As a kid he looks up to gangsters who have their headquarters across the street from his parents' apartment, admiring the fact that they don't have to obey the normal rules. His father is too busy working to pay much attention to him, other than the odd angry outburst, so he turns to the mob guys for recognition and undergoes a form of initiation into manhood when he's busted by the police for selling hijacked goods but says nothing. His mob allegiance seems a natural process. His euphoria at being welcomed by the guys after the trial is nicely captured by the use of an upbeat rendition of the pop song "Sometimes I wonder why I spend the lonely hours dreaming of a song" and the shot of an airplane rising quickly beyond the telephone lines. Scorsese's use of pop music is effective here where, at other times, it begins to seem like wall-to-wall carpeting. Still, it's the music of wise-guy culture: raw, sentimental, florid, and frequent. The odd thing is that Scorsese doesn't place it in the dramatic space. A radio is not always, or sometimes, playing. It has the feeling of being laid on. Its frequency can be explained by Scorsese's need to keep the fast-paced rhythm of the narration going.

From the beginning Henry is a tender-hearted fellow, attempting as a youngster to help a local guy who's been shot near the headquarters, to the irritation of the gangsters who say they've got to toughen him up. This "softness" causes him problems as a full-fledged member of the crew. He's even feminized in his makeup, through the subtle use of eye liner. He never becomes hardened to the violence he witnesses. In this way, he's our representative in the film and a direct heir of the character of J.R. (Harvey Keitel) in *Mean Streets*. He doesn't have J.R.'s complex moral sense, but he's still the man in the middle. He mediates between the hard guys like

Jimmie and Tommy and their prey. This is most clearly seen in the case of Morrie, the wig man, and Jimmie. Morrie is a compulsive gambler who's in constant need of money which he tries to obtain by badgering Jimmie, who's charging him exorbitant rates for loans. Henry tries to keep Morrie off Jimmie's back, knowing what could happen to Morrie. It's Morrie who comes up with the plan to rob a shipment of cash at Kennedy Airport which brings the crew six million dollars. Jimmie's refusal to pay Morrie his share sends him over the edge and brings on Jimmie's decision to kill him. Significantly, Jimmie tells Henry the murder is canceled and then immediately has Tommy put an ice pick in the back of Morrie's head. He's deflecting Henry from his mission of compassion because he knows he might warn Morrie. Henry's kindness is tolerated by Jimmie and Tommy, perhaps even valued as a way they wish they could be if they didn't have to do what they do. He's their mascot. He's surprised and shocked at the murder of Stacks, the black member of the crew, immediately after the Kennedy robbery. He doesn't see that Jimmie has plans for the whole crew. His naïveté seems quaint; but he may be more cunning than it appears, using his naïveté because he knows it protects him.

He clearly is reckless in his drug dealing and addiction. His laughter at Tommy's crude, violent jokes becomes more hysterical as the film goes on. He's out of control with Sandy, who manages to snort even more cocaine than he does. He lies to Paulie about his dealing. He lies regularly to Karen about his mistresses. He'd be surprised to run across someone who's not on the take. His deviousness is just standard procedure in a business where payoffs to police, judges, and jail guards are a way of life. He turns on Paulie and Jimmie only because he knows they plan to kill him. Again, it's just business.

But it's family business. This is the chief irony of the film. All the family dinners, vacations, embraces (the guys are always hugging each other and giving affectionate kisses on the cheek) don't disguise the fact that it's your closest member of the extended family who may do you in. As Henry says as he goes to Jimmie for their last meeting in a diner: "There are no disputes, arguments or curses like in the movies. Friends, people who've cared for you all of your life, kill you by coming at you with a smile when you're at your weakest and most in need of their help." Family love and loyalty is both real (Karen's passionate devotion to her family) and a fiction (Jimmie's decision to get rid of Henry). It's not merely just business; the illegality makes everyone aware that his friend could begin to cooperate with the authorities. The "family values" dimension of *The Godfather* is reinterpreted here.

In this respect, Paulie is not the avuncular caretaker of the family. As played with dark majesty by Paul Sorvino, he's a stern—even forbidding—man who's quite capable of ordering killings of close confederates to preserve his power. Also, he's always cooking or eating. When Henry comes to him for the last time, he has a skillet full of sausages in front of him. And he's very particular about the menu they prepare for each other in prison: pasta, steak, lobster, wine—ingredients sent past the bribed guards. The tribute he collects from various robberies should make him a wealthy man, but he lives in a nondescript house in a working-class part of town and his headquarters is in back of a local market. He has none of the baronial trappings of Don Corleone in *The Godfather*. He's an old-style boss who prefers hijacking, loan-sharking, and protection to drug dealing. He doesn't order Henry's death, though he knows he may turn on him and, as a result, dies in prison as he tells Henry he fears doing. His warnings to Henry about Jimmie and Tommy suggest that he has a special feeling for him, perhaps like a son. If this is true, it costs him dearly. Like the others, he wants to take care of Henry.

Tommy, as played by Joe Pesci, is the wild man of the crew. He's loud and aggressive and quick to violence. Underneath, he is insecure. "He's a cowboy who has too much to prove," Paulie warns Henry. He likes to tell jokes laced with violence, and even though the jokes aren't very funny they provoke raucous laughter. He likes to bully. His insistent questioning when Henry tells him he's funny ("Funny how?") is pure intimidation. He's attached to his mother, played by Scorsese's mother, and seems to have trouble getting women, since he likes the attractive Henry to go along on double dates. It's his mother who helps him get ready for the ceremony of becoming a "made man" in the mob. His execution is nicely presented. As he enters the room in which the ceremony is to occur, the camera holds a couple of beats on the empty room. It's not a point-of-view shot, but its duration approximates the time it takes for Tommy to realize he's been set up. At the end of the shot he murmurs, "Oh no," before receiving a bullet in the head. His killing of Billy Batts, a made man in the Gambino organization, has finally caught up with him. His murder of the boy, Spider, who gets drinks for the card players, is one of the most horrifying moments in the film. He has wounded Spider a few weeks earlier by shooting him in the foot. He's a movie buff and wants to reenact the scene from "The Oklahoma Kid" in which one cowboy makes another dance by shooting at his feet. Now he continues to bully him until Spider tells him, "Fuck you." At first Tommy sits quietly but Jimmie provokes him by laughing at him and asking what he's going to do about Spider's insult. After the shooting, he grabs the gun and calls Tommy crazy, but it's a craziness he's known about all along and, in a sense, he's as responsible for Spider's death as Tommy. Tommy, for all his wildness, is as much a part of the culture as the rest of them. In a quieter sequence, we see him and the others sitting in the Copacabana in rapt, open-mouthed attention to the sentimental singing of "Pretend You Don't See Her, My Heart" by Jerry Vale. The violent and the sentimental go hand in hand.

Jimmie is Tommy's opposite: cold and cunning. He's not as personally violent as Tommy, but he's more ruthless. De Niro's Sam "Ace" Rothstein and Pesci's Nicky Santoro in *Casino* are essentially the same roles in the same relationship. Jimmie has every member of the six million dollar Kennedy crew killed, not only because they start spending money right away and thus tip off the authorities, but because he wants to keep the money. He's willing to join Henry in going behind Paulie's back in drug dealing because of the money. We never see him in the group at the Copacabana; he's all business. De Niro's subtle, controlled performance stands in sharp contrast to Pesci's flamboyance as Tommy. Jimmie's calculating nature is well presented in a brief four-shot sequence when he stands at the bar smoking and decides to kill Morrie. Henry has calmed the out-of-control Morrie down, lightening his mood even into song before the sequence begins. In shot one Henry gives a worried look at Jimmie. In two we see a close up of Jimmie at the bar. He's smoking and has a preoccupied look as he turns his head. Shot 3 shows us the object of Jimmie's glance as Morrie, singing, walks toward the camera. In 4, the longest, we have a medium shot of Jimmie. He has the slightest smile which continues to grow as the camera closes in and a propulsive rock music enters the soundtrack. He's made up his mind about Morrie. The power of De Niro's acting here comes from understatement. We see this again in his final meeting with Henry in the diner. He's wearing glasses which slightly enlarge his eyes. When he asks Henry to go to Florida for a job we're given a freeze-frame of his face. His pale blue eyes are calm and cold. Henry tells us in voice-over that he knows Jimmie will have him killed. He is thrilled when he learns that Tommy will become a made man and terribly distraught when he learns that Tommy has been killed. Like Henry, he can't become made because he's part Irish; he views Tommy's opportunity as his own. Such warmth is rare from him. Behind De Niro's patented fox-like smile is a cruel will. Karen experiences his implied threat in a powerful sequence in which he sends her down the block from his warehouse to pick out some (stolen) Dior dresses for herself. His manner is kind and avuncular, but he won't walk down with her; and when she looks into the door, she sees the back-lit figure of a man lifting boxes and decides to leave. It is not likely Jimmie is going to harm her here—he hasn't dealt with Henry yet—but the subtle danger is there and it is real.

One of the most interesting sequences in the film, however brief, is the killing of Stacks which is presented in four shots. In shot 1 we see him asleep in bed, there's a knock on the door and he gets up, Tommy enters and follows him into the bedroom, remarking that Stacks isn't with "one of your bitches" (the prejudice against blacks is a constant on the part of the mob in the film). Tommy circles behind Stacks and shoots him in the back of the head, blood flashing forward onto the white bed sheets. In shot 2 Tommy's companion Frank Carbone stands nonplussed in the doorway and we hear three more shots before they leave. So far the sequence has the matter-of-fact directness of the killing by Travis Bickle of the black robber in the little neighborhood market in *Taxi Driver*. But Scorsese adds two shots. In number 3 the screen is completely black until we see Tommy's black coat move away from the camera. The pop music of the Christmas song which has accompanied Henry and Karen's Christmas celebration (which preceded Stacks' murder) returns and we have an upward angled shot in slow motion as Tommy fires down five times (a continuity error?). Henry's voice-over explains that Stacks had failed to get rid of the truck used in the Kennedy robbery and that the police had found it and therefore Stacks had to be killed before the police arrive. Shot 4 shows Stacks lying dead next to his bloody bed. Why do we see Stacks' killing twice? Henry's explanation doesn't account for the repetition. The emphasis, particularly in the slow-motion shot 3, is upon Tommy the romanticized killer.

In our last view of Henry, he's living in a nondescript tract house, perhaps in the South. He complains that he's no longer like "a movie star with muscle," that there's "no action," and that "I'm an average nobody who gets to live the rest of my life like a schnook." But he looks healthy and free of drugs as he smiles at the camera. His fondness for his former life is summed up with a shot of Tommy shooting directly at the viewer. Given Henry's repugnance at Tommy's violence, this shot seems out of character. It's like Scorsese's repetition in slow motion of Tommy's murder of Stacks. The final shot of Tommy is not from Henry but from Scorsese, who cast his own mother as Tommy's mother. Tommy the movie buff is Scorsese here. For Scorsese, Tommy's gun play remains exciting and romantic. The youthful attraction to the tough guy hasn't changed.[1]

Note

1. David Thomson's comment that "Scorsese is the adult version of a delicate hypersensitive kid who grew up in a rough neighborhood and ever afterwards felt bound to pretend that he was a hit man as well as a violinist," is worth noting. *A Biographical Dictionary of Film* (New York: Knopf, 1994), 678.

Chapter 13

PRELUDE TO RAPE

CAPE FEAR, 1991

Cape Fear marks a major shift in Scorsese's career. It is a successful attempt at a blockbuster and shows it. He decided to do an adaptation of J. Lee Thompson's highly successful *Cape Fear* (1962), based on the novel *The Executioners* by John MacDonald. As agreed with Universal Studios and Steven Spielberg, he would have a large budget. Scorsese's film is a kind of homage to the older film. Gregory Peck, Robert Mitchum, and Martin Balsam, main actors in Thompson's film, make cameo appearances. Most importantly, the powerful film score by Bernard Herrmann is used again, with only minor changes by Elmer Bernstein. The script by Wesley Shick is adapted to more contemporary concerns, though it follows the basic plot of the original. Scorsese's *Cape Fear* is an inflated, gaudy version, however. It's as if he said to himself, "Well, I'm really going to pull out all the stops and make a popular hit; I'm going to grab the widest audience and make them scream." The film accomplished its goal; it made millions for Disney and proved that Scorsese could make a hit—but at what cost. Of all his films, *Cape Fear* bears Scorsese's signature the least. It's full of crude formulas, guaranteed to please a wide public. At times the film even seems to be a baroque parody of the original. It's entertaining in a heavy-handed way, but many viewers who know it prefer the older film. Like *The Color of Money*, the only other adaptation of a successful film, it isn't as good as the original though both films served to prove to Hollywood's money men that Scorsese could score at the box office.

The story involves the unceasing terrorizing of Sam and Leigh Bowden and their daughter, Danielle, by a crazed convict, Max Cady. Cady (Robert De Niro) has discovered in prison that his defense attorney Sam (Nick Nolte) withheld evidence that might have shortened his sentence for rape and sexual battery. After fourteen years in prison he dedicates himself to punishing Sam and his family. Cady is an odd—even unreal—mixture of fanaticism and subtle, perceptive intelligence. He's both a self-absorbed monomaniac and a person capable of canceling his own obsessions and registering the minutest cracks and fissures in the people he pursues. He nearly wrecks Sam's legal career, almost seduces Danielle, and comes close to raping her and Leigh (Jessica Lange) in a houseboat on the river, Cape Fear, where the family has fled to escape from him. He finally dies when the houseboat breaks up on the rocks and the family is washed up barely alive on the shore.

In the not very subtle subtext, Cady is the nightmare figure produced by guilty acts. He's a messenger from the underworld who breaks into the "perfection" of middle-class respectability. And Sam has plenty to be guilty about. In an updating of the nice family in the first *Cape Fear*, the Bowdens live in a rich, handsome house, but they are in trouble. Sam cheats on his wife, withholds evidence, and tries harshly to keep the lid on the rebellious, sexually curious Danielle (Juliette Lewis). Leigh has become cynical about Sam; she craves excitement. She and Sam fight a lot. Danielle, who is more aware of sex and marijuana than her parents suspect or want her to be, feels that they don't want her to grow up. She feels she's living in a hypocritical world where grownups say one thing and do another. Cady exploits a preternatural insight into each family member as he terrorizes them.

De Niro's performance as Cady is nearly "over the top," as the phrase has it today. Unlike Mitchum, who remains cool and cunning, De Niro gives a nearly operatic performance: singing, preaching, joking, performing a variety of roles. He's covered with tatoos: biblical quotations on his arms ("vengeance is mine," "my time is at hand"), a massive depiction of the scales of justice on his back. He's been pumping iron in prison and his body has the musculature of a body builder, right down to the washboard stomach. De Niro, who has always acted with his body as much as his voice, here shows another transformation—the opposite of the flabby, overweight fighter in *Raging Bull*. In the early scenes he approaches Sam with joking hostility. He likes to play with his victims before he assaults them. Sam's pretense to his wife, to a fellow lawyer, and to Cady that he doesn't remember the Cady rape case may actually be true. He's conveniently buried his corrupt part in the case as he has forgotten other transgressions in his life. He's the average, middle-class, short-cutting man, trying to skim through life in a pleasant way. Cady confronts him with his guilt and manipulates him with it expertly. In a heavy-handed sequence at the end of the film, Sam, having nearly killed Cady with a large rock, finds his hands covered with blood which he attempts to wash away.

The violence in the older *Cape Fear* is as much implied as explicit, but in Scorsese's film it is fully acted out and lurid. Nothing is left to the imagination. As in the formulaic stalker films, the violence is almost entirely directed at women. Cady's assault on Lori, the law clerk with whom Sam is beginning an affair, is a good example. Lori seems to find the whole incident amusing, right down to the moment Cady begins to brutalize her. She even laughs when he puts handcuffs on her. There is the implication that in her stupidity, neediness, and drunkenness, she's asked for what she's getting. The actual assault is a horror: Cady bites a large chunk of flesh from her cheek. He's not interested in sex, but in inflicting pain. She refuses to testify against him because she knows she'll be put on trial. She's a later version of the rape victim from whom Sam defended Cady. The evidence Sam withheld is that the woman had three lovers in the month before Cady attacked her. Her promiscuity, like Lori's, means she had it coming. In her thirst for excitement, Leigh is like these women. After she and Sam make love, she gets out of bed in the middle of the night and puts on lipstick, sensuously brushing her lips with her fingers (a gesture she repeats on the houseboat when threatened with rape by Cady). She's unsatisfied. Part of her welcomes the possibility of rape, even as she resists it. Her daughter, Danielle, repeats her mother's gesture of brushing her lips when Cady looms over her on the houseboat. She is sexually precocious and adventure-seeking. The film comes close to asserting that all women have rape fantasies and like to move toward the borderline in which they might be acted out. In its crude understanding of female behavior, the film reveals its sexist bias and opens Scorsese to the charge of misogyny. Unfortunately it's a charge which has some merit. From the overly compliant young woman in *Who's That Knocking at My Door?* (she's known only as "the girl," played by Zina Bethune), to the objectified Teresa (Amy Robinson) in *Mean Streets*, to the domination of Iris (Jodie Foster) by Sport and the seductive bitchiness of Betsy (Cybill Shepherd) in *Taxi Driver*, to the crude and often violent manipulation of Vickie (Cathy Moriarty) by Jake in *Raging Bull*, to the series of threatening, destructive women in *After Hours*, the disturbing pattern emerges of women either hostile or dominated and abused by men who seem to be acting on the assumption that they must pursue their destinies, women be damned. There are few strong, assertive women in Scorsese's films (Karen played by Lorraine Bracco in *Goodfellas* is one). Most are subservient to the driven man in their lives, even when they themselves are gifted, as in Francine Evans (Liza Minnelli) in *New York, New York*. They are more than victims; they deserve what's coming to them. This pattern is seen most flagrantly in *Cape Fear*, a film which presents an extended prelude to rape as just plain old entertainment.

The lurid, lip-smacking violence of *Cape Fear* is another problem. It is not only titillating but unreal. Cady gets up after a brutal battering by three men who've been hired to "warn" him, and lays them out one by one. He's indestructible in the manner of the hero of a Western or kung fu movie. This is violence for the fun of it, not the traumatic, honest violence of *Mean Streets* or *Taxi Driver*. In those films, Scorsese's depiction of violence has a naked forcefulness that, however disturbing, has integrity. Travis Bickle's rampage at the end of *Taxi Driver* is memorable because of the authenticity of its presentation. The violence in *Cape Fear* dissolves in the mind because it is so much like other movies. In this sense, even though he's just playing around with popular entertainment, Scorsese violates his own artistic integrity.

Many film lovers avoid Scorsese's films because of their violence. It's an irony that his best films' treatment of violence in *Mean Streets, Taxi Driver,* and *Raging Bull* failed to draw crowds, while *Cape Fear* played to packed houses. A far better treatment of compulsive violence against women is *Silence of the Lambs,* in which we see few scenes of actual violence. The violence is implied in Anthony Hopkins' ferociously restrained performance, which enables the viewer to imagine a violence perhaps more horrifying than what could be portrayed. *Cape Fear,* by comparison, is both too literal and too grandiloquent. We're not repelled and fascinated at the same time by the violence in the film as we are in *Taxi Driver* or even *The King of Comedy. Cape Fear*'s presentation uses the standardized attitude of making violence both scary and fun, of saying it is both terrible and amusing. It's another indication that Americans like a heavy serving of violence but don't like it straight.

The formula-like nature of the film can also be seen in some of its most minute cinematic strategies. Shots often begin with a burst of sound to increase excitement: the slamming of a door, the roaring of a car engine, the slamming of the judge's gavel as he imposes a restraining order on Sam. Scorsese also uses many loud sound splices to link shots. There's a lot of "in-your-face" camera work: Cady walks right into the camera when he gets out of prison; the bodies and ball go right at the camera in the violent racquetball sequence. The lighting of many shots is ambient bright with few or no shadows—the kind of lighting we're used to in many of the more wholesome Disney films. One wonders whether Scorsese didn't get a bit bored with these formulas and decide to inflate them. The film is an homage, but it also has the feel of a comic-book parody of the understated original.

The excessiveness of *Cape Fear* is best seen in the houseboat segment which takes up about a quarter of the running time. Scorsese gets carried away with the special effects his big budget allowed him. There are many shots of the houseboat (using miniatures) swirling out of control, breaking up on the rocks, and other shots of the interior twisting and turning wildly as the actors, or their doubles, are tossed around. In this hypercharged environment, Cady makes his final attack on the Bowdens. The camera moves wildly, sometimes rolling completely over and around; the soundtrack of storm and music is overwhelming. Cady, having been soaked in lighter fluid and set on fire, leaps overboard and then reappears fully functional as his hand emerges out of the tossing water to grab the frayed boat line. This, and the repeated preparations for raping the women, goes on for quite a while. It is an orgy that finally didn't happen.

There are two good reasons to see *Cape Fear*: the performance by Juliette Lewis as Danielle and De Niro in one scene in particular, and Bernard Herrmann's score. The lengthy scene between Danielle and Cady in the high school theater is the high point of the film and, in its quiet intensity, contrasts sharply with the rest of the film. In a phone call to Danielle the night before, Cady has presented himself as her new drama teacher. In Scorsese's treatment, he is hanging upside-down on one of his body building machines as he talks. The next day he meets her on the stage set of the little house in the woods. He is smoking a joint and eventually persuades her to take a puff. He tells her he knows she's unhappy that her parents won't let her grow up, that they're punishing her for sins they used to commit, like smoking marijuana. He uses the teacherly language of theater as an arena of self-discovery. His sympathetic insight wins her over, even as he says jokingly, "I'm the big bad wolf from the black forest." He puts his arm around her, then puts his thumb in her mouth, and finally deeply kisses her before he walks away. De Niro's performance here is mesmerizing; he's like a cunning pedophile. He evokes Cady's evil more powerfully here than in the action-oriented sequences. His power is mental; he can mirror his prey's innermost feelings and use them to manipulate her. Juliette Lewis' face registers Danielle's movement from anxiety to doubt to trust to fear with astonishing accuracy. She believes she's found an older person who really understands her and wants to help her grow, but he moves so lightly and so fast that he penetrates her defenses almost before she knows it. In a sense, she's been raped without knowing it.

The Herrmann score is simplicity itself: based on four descending notes in full brass chorus, with strings coming in behind in an echoing descent. It's somewhat like his score for *Taxi Driver*. The effect is powerful and threatening, as if Cady's revenge cannot be stopped. An interesting use occurs during the parade sequence. This cheerful, all-American event on a sunny day is undercut by the music, which matches the rhythm of overhead shots of the marchers. It's as if Scorsese is saying that underneath the celebration a destructive force is working that must move forward.

Chapter 14

A LIFE UNLIVED

THE AGE OF INNOCENCE, 1993

Scorsese's next choice of subject was the furthest imaginable from the excesses of *Cape Fear*. *The Age of Innocence* is a study of sexual repression in the narrow confines of upper-class society in the New York City of the 1870s. Commonly regarded as Edith Wharton's finest novel, *The Age of Innocence* confronted Scorsese with the task of adapting a classic American literary text. Most directors like to avoid such projects because a free cinematic reinvention, like Jane Campion's fine treatment of Henry James' *Portrait of a Lady*, tends to be regarded as a debasement of the work of literature. They're tied too closely to the literary text and, in the case of a novel, are under the obligation to cram it all into a two- or two-and-a-half-hour space. Scorsese's and Jay Cocks' adaptation is very fine;

it does justice to the novel without feeling like a visual imprint of it. Most of all, in its new subject and style, it reveals the breadth of Scorsese's creative sensibility and his range as a director.

The decision to use a voice-over narrator (Joanne Woodward reading from the novel's text) both honors Wharton's novel as a work of literature and adds complexity to the cinematic text. As I plan to argue, the narrative voice often undercuts the visuals, giving many sequences a subtle irony. The usual presentation of upper-class life in adaptations of literary classics (Jane Austen, E. M. Forster, Henry James) emphasizes the glamorous opulence of the surroundings. The characters may have problems, but they aren't ones of survival. Scorsese's film is opulent as well, but it's an opulence for which one pays a price. Wharton knew the narrowness and moral rigidity of upper-class New York society into which she was born; she left it for good and went to live in France. The subject of *The Age of Innocence* is the cost to Newland Archer of staying.

Archer (Daniel Day-Lewis) is a successful lawyer and connoisseur of the arts. Unlike many of his friends, he isn't interested mainly in money making or in social gossip. He is a kind of outsider who performs the social rituals of his class without fully assenting to them (or so he believes). He'd just as soon stay at home in the evening and read. His meeting the Countess Ellen Olenska (Michelle Pfeiffer) nearly throws his planned marriage to May Welland (Winona Ryder) on the rocks. May is entirely conventional; but Ellen, who is separated from a decadent European count, awakens Archer's dormant energies. Though they never consummate their affair, the rest of New York society assumes they have; and after Ellen returns to Europe, Archer is left in a compromised position. He raises a family with May and achieves great success in the law but remains, at the end, essentially unfulfilled. Capable of real passion, as so many of his friends are not, he has lived his life unable to act on it.

Scorsese took special pains to establish an authentic period atmosphere through his production designer, Dante Ferretti, right down to the conical mounding of snow in the streets in an era before snow removal equipment. The opulent interiors are carefully designed to evoke each character; they aren't lavish for the sake of lavishness. The lingering shots of silver place settings, flower arrangements, wedding gifts, and artistically presented food evoke the sumptuous conventions of the period, but there's a sameness to them. There's always a "roman punch" on the table. There's not much invention and not much enthusiasm in the consumption. The paintings are particularly important. There's a coarse richness to the furnishings of the man-about-town Julius Beaufort's house as the camera follows Archer from room to room in an early sequence. The camera glances up several times at Beaufort's paintings, particularly a "scandalous" study of a nude woman and infants, the "Return of Spring," by Bougereau. The works of art worth collecting are French or at least continental, certainly not American.

The narrative voice takes on particular weight as we accompany Archer in a visit to the Van der Luydens, the highest arbiters of New York society: they "dwelled above in a kind of supraterrestrial twilight . . . they have an exquisitely refined sense of tribal order." These words are uttered with a reverential hush. The Van der Luydens' house is indeed opulent, though austere by Beaufort's standards. As the camera pulls back from the couch on which the hosts sit, we see a series of dull family portraits in subdued colors (the Van der Luydens themselves are dressed in black). The narrator's words serve to subvert the rich setting: these people are snobs of the deepest order; they may be kindly but they are also stuffed shirts to whom others pay homage. The dinner they give for a visiting duke is another example. As the overhead camera scans the colorful table (the food actually looks tasty), we're told that such a dinner is given with "religious solemnity." It's an ornate event, lavish but dull. None of the diners seems to be having much fun. This is the society from which Archer unknowingly wishes to escape. He is surprised at his laughing agreement when Ellen calls the Van der Luydens dull, and he's intrigued when she says it seems odd that America would struggle for independence from Europe only to try to "become a copy of another country." His ambivalent attitude toward her is indicated in the opening sequence at the opera when he hesitates to take her hand when they're introduced: he's attracted to her and wary about her because of her reputation as a fallen woman. He is frightened of the freedom she might release in him.

A basic technique in the film has the camera lingering over a social ritual while the narrator speaks. The final dinner sequence involves a party the Archers give for Ellen just before she leaves. In a representative shot, the camera remains overhead, withdrawing very slowly as the narrator tells us that Archer views his guests as conspirators who have separated him and Ellen and enforced the tribal laws which now imprison him. The irony here is that Archer is at least as responsible for his situation as his enforcers, though he can't admit it. He hasn't been able to make a break with society as Ellen has. He is aware of his passivity when he ruefully tells her earlier, "I'm the man who married one woman because another told him to. . . .You gave me my first glimpse of a real life and then told me to carry on with a false one. No one can endure that." Her reply, "I am enduring it," indicates her strength. She's way ahead of him. She asks him if he'd want her as a mistress and he replies, "I want to find a world where words like that don't exist," to which she laughs, "Where is that country? Have you ever been there?" Archer is most a part of New York society's puritanical naïveté here. He's the undeveloped man of his time. Still, he is far finer than the men who surround him. If he were not so, he'd have an easier time of it, skimming through life like Beaufort, or Laurence Lefferts, or Sillerton Jackson. In another representative shot, the camera slowly makes several complete turns in Archer's study as the narrative voice tells us that he continued to live most of his life in this room, raising his children, watching them grow up, losing May to an early death, pursuing his legal career. As the camera pivots, the changing furnishings of the room mark the passage of time, as well as represent the luxurious confinement which has entrapped him.

More should be said about the film's use of paintings. Every interior in the film has carefully chosen paintings which evoke the owner. They are extensions of the sensibility of the collectors, statements about their social attitudes. Mrs. Manson Mingott, May's grandmother, who surrounds her prostrate self with lap dogs, has lots of paintings of dogs and landscapes at sunset. She may be high-spirited and outspoken, but she's entirely conventional. Beaufort's Bougereau nude is an advertisement of his rakishness; the Van der Luydens' portraits stress their august ancestry. Archer, who is always looking at paintings wherever he goes, is not interested in these works. He is, however, by the paintings he sees at Ellen's. The first is a kind of pre-Impressionist image of a woman with a parasol sitting by a lake, her face a simple patch of flesh tone without features. The next is an Italian or French landscape in clear southern light on a very long horizontal canvas. The camera pans slowly along the frame as Archer studies it. They are new works to him, new ways of seeing, and they increase his fascination with Ellen. In a later scene between them at Ellen's, Archer stands at the fireplace next to a painting of a young nude boy and a cheetah. The erotic element is stronger at this point; Archer's interest has intensified. It's as if Ellen's paintings have touched his body as well as his mind. His own paintings aren't so sensual; his prized possession is one of J. M. W. Turner's semi-abstract river scenes, a painting which in the 1870s would be regarded as shockingly modern. He also has paintings of Egypt and the pyramids. His choices are both radical and conventional; they express him very well. He's an aesthete but not a creator, a man with a curious mind who's content to do his explorations in his study, looking at books of Japanese prints, reading modern poetry. Perhaps the closest he comes to artistic creativity is in his dandified style of dress, his ornately decorated evening robes which he wears in his study. Paintings are one way for him to engage the world from a distance without having to risk himself. Paintings even tell him who he is, as when he returns as an old man to Paris and stands in front of a massive Rubens canvas in the Louvre, full of writing passionate flesh. The voice-over tells us that Ellen now stands for all that he had missed and that he thinks of her "abstractly, serenely, like an imaginary loved one in a book or picture." In a sense, he's put her in a painting in order to diminish her power. And we actually see this process when they meet surreptitiously in Boston just before she leaves. As he enters the park where he finds her, he notices a painter doing some detailed brushwork on a figure sitting on a bench. He scrutinizes this figure (we never see the whole painting, only a close-up of the figure) and then glances up to see that it is Ellen on the bench. She's in "his" painting even before they say goodbye. As in *Life Lessons*, Scorsese is using paintings to evoke the inner man.

The film itself by and large avoids painterly shots. It wants to present the period without succumbing to its visual clichés. The major exception is the novel's famous scene when Archer approaches and then turns back from Ellen as she's standing on the dock at Mrs. Manson Mingott's. This sequence is filmed in a suffused, roseate light with the sun flashing off the water as a sailboat passes the lighthouse on the point. It's a very romantic, effulgent scene, suitable for hanging on the wall. The absence of point of view shots makes it unclear that the ripeness is a product of Archer's own painterly romanticism. A more powerful image occurs when Archer approaches Ellen, again from the rear, to help her into her coat before she says goodbye for good. The camera's slow approach to the warm flesh of her bare shoulders and neck evokes Archer's balked passion very well.

Two passages evoking this passion are worth looking at. The first is the seven-shot sequence in which Archer, riding in a carriage with Ellen, kisses her wrist. It's one of the cinematic high points. The first four shots are brief renderings in close-up of Archer's hands as he unbuttons Ellen's glove. The rhythm of the shots is both sensually languorous and anticipatory. The next three shots show his head as it moves down to her hand and his lips as they touch her naked upturned wrist. It's a very sexy, passionate sequence. The next passage is more full of fantasy: Archer imagines that Ellen has come up behind him and put her arms around his neck as they pass the day alone in a house in the country. In six shots, Scorsese evokes the power of Archer's imagination. We see close-ups of Ellen's hands as she approaches, then a shot of her hands sliding over his shoulders and down his chest, then a shot as he slowly moves his head back in ecstasy, then a shot as he turns his head in alarm to see Ellen sitting some distance away. Significantly, he imagines her as the active lover.

Ellen's role as depicted by Scorsese and Cocks is more aggressive than in the novel. She flirts openly with Archer, though she knows he is engaged to her cousin, at one point surprising him with the declaration that they'll meet at five the next day. Gossipy New York society immediately picks up on her moves and relishes the prospect of seeing the decorous Archer compromised. She puts him in a tough spot right away, but it is a spot he wants to be in. She's more than a little disingenuous when she tells Archer she's been unaware how society has regarded her own position as a not-quite-divorced woman. She wants to act freely, to go out openly with Beaufort and see Archer quietly, and let society think what it will. Yet she's scrupulous when it comes to her love for Archer; she won't be his mistress and she won't return to the count, saying, "I can't love you unless I give you up." She can only love him in a state of nearly religious renunciation. It's the Jamesean note, echoed by Wharton.

Beneath her girlish sweetness and conventionality, May is very tough. She deflects Archer's two attempts to tell her of his love for Ellen because she knows she's won. She means to preserve her marriage at any price, including accepting a husband she knows doesn't deeply love her. Her story to their son Ted, that she asked Archer to sacrifice what he loved best, isn't really accurate; it is her romantic picture. She is willing to stretch the truth about her pregnancy to Ellen in order to stop the affair. The shots of Winona Ryder's smiling, happy face toward the end of the film are full of triumph, but also aggression. Archer's opinion of her, as the narrator makes clear, is one of barely concealed condescension: she has "great depth of feeling . . . with an absence of imagination"; it is useless to try "to emancipate a woman who had no notion she was not free"; her "hard, bright blindness" causes "her incapacity to recognize change." In his superiority, he blames her for the conventionality he has settled for. She, at least, saw danger and acted to remove it.

Archer's put-down of May isn't validated by Scorsese in the usual pattern of his treatment of women. His remarks serve unconsciously to condemn his own behavior. Ellen is much stronger than he. Along with Karen in *Goodfellas*, she's the strongest woman in the films. Her character is, of course, more Wharton's invention than Scorsese's.

Archer is a wistful, dried-up man at the end. He is fifty-seven and walks with a stoop. In the intimate space of the Place Fürstemberg in

Paris, he can't bring himself to visit Ellen. He prefers to keep the faded picture he has of her rather than to see her in the present. Though he has prospered and raised a family, it is as if an essential part of his life stopped long ago. In this sense, he's like many men and women who have feared to take the risk of acting on their passions when these passions went strongly against convention or economic safety. He's had a good life, but not the life he could have had.

Chapter 15

THE MOB AGAIN

CASINO, 1995

Having demonstrated his creative range with *The Age of Innocence,* Scorsese evidently felt the need in *Casino* to return to the familiar subject of the mob, treated so well in *Goodfellas. Casino* (1995) is very long—179 minutes, to be exact—and it feels like a long film. For the first time in his career, Scorsese repeats himself, even down to specific shots and sequences. There's a feeling of exhaustion behind the film's gaudiness and inflation. It's as if he has run out of things to say.

The subject of *Casino* is the last days of the mob in Las Vegas, before the big corporations take over. The script by Scorsese and Nicholas Pileggi is tied very closely to Pileggi's book of the same title. The two major characters are designed to dramatize the two aspects of mob control:

Sam "Ace" Rothstein (De Niro) is the new-style businessman mobster sent by the bosses to run the new Tangiers casino; Nicky Santoro (Joe Pesci) is the old-style thug who freely uses violence. He's also been sent out by the bosses. Ace and Nicky are old mob friends, and the story of their disintegrating loyalty is also the history of the last days of the mob in Las Vegas. *Casino* is also a retelling of *Mean Streets*, with Ace in the role of Charlie, the compromised figure who tries to keep his friend Johnny Boy under control. De Niro has moved from his revved-up Johnny Boy to a later version of the well-meaning Charlie, as played by Harvey Keitel in *Mean Streets*, and Pesci as Nicky has stepped into De Niro's role of the trouble maker. The film alternates between sections of Ace's and Nicky's voice-over narration.

The opening choral passages from Bach's *St. Matthew Passion*, which accompany the credits, suggest that we're about to witness a drama with religious implications. But *Mean Streets* is easier to see as a drama of souls than is *Casino*. If Nicky is purely evil, the aggressive instinct without a governor, Ace is not good. He's as much a product of the mob as Nicky, who at least does his own killing. They're two sides of the same coin: one the "respectable" money maker, the other the brutal enforcer. The coin is minted in Las Vegas and the best parts of the film, about the first forty-five minutes, are a semi-documentary about how the Tangiers operates under the mob. With Ace as narrator, we are given a tour of the casino and shown how it works. In a seven-shot sequence the camera follows a man with a suitcase (he is identified as a Mormon) as he enters the count room where, amazingly enough, the paper money is counted by hand and the silver held in small galvanized buckets until they are emptied into a machine which counts and packages them. The "skim" is explained by Ace as the man fills the suitcase with bills, then takes a private jet to Kansas City where he hands over the money to the big bosses who are gathered in the back of a small, nondescript Italian grocery store. This money avoids federal and state taxes. The bosses can run Las Vegas, we're told, because they control Teamsters' pension fund monies. The organization is explained by brief shots of the big boss, Remo Gaggi; Andy Stone, head of the pension fund; and Philip Green, the figurehead chairman of the Tangiers Corporation. We watch Ginger, Ace's future wife, practice her hustle, giving her clients "lucky pills"—speed—to enable them to stay up for days and thus gamble and lose more. The camera even gives us a close-up shot of Ginger's hands as she folds a one hundred dollar bill in a special way and palms it in order to pass it on to a valet parking attendant who will bribe the local cops to keep away from her. It's a brief "how-to-do-it" sequence, and it enforces Ace's remark that Las Vegas is "kickback city." We watch two card cheats get busted by Ace and his security staff—an electric cattle prod in the armpit to simulate a heart attack at the table and then a series of hammer blows to the hand in the back room. A wealthy Asian gambler, who steals the hotel towels, wins hugely at Baccarat and is tricked into returning to the tables, where he ends up a loser. These sequences are fast and economical in the way they show the casino's methods. Perhaps no film better shows Scorsese's documentary impulse. But the film repeats the *Goodfellas* story in a Las Vegas setting. The long documentary opening is brisk and amusing, like the first part of *Goodfellas*; the latter half turns darker and more violent as the mob disintegrates again like its predecessor. Ace, like Henry Hill, somehow survives, speaking to the camera in the final shot. *Casino* is thus like *The Color of Money* and *Cape Fear*, an adaptation of an earlier film—but not a film by someone else. It wasn't made under the pressure to prove to the money men that Scorsese could produce a commercial product, like the earlier films. *Goodfellas* was very successful at the box office. In *Casino* Scorsese seems to be treading water. His defensiveness in interviews about the film, as quoted by Lawrence Friedman, acknowledges the defects of repetition.[1] Why, we might ask, is Scorsese so attracted to mob behavior? Les Keyser's excellent description of Scorsese's youth provides an answer.[2] A small sickly boy growing up in a rough neighborhood, he couldn't hold his own in fights, but he could take punishment without running away and the tougher kids let up on him because of his asthma. He looked up to these toughs and to the mob guys who often were their fathers. He also escaped the threat of the street by going to movies, some of which celebrated gangster life as well as the macho gun play in the many Westerns he saw. These movies captured his imagination, and he would return home and draw crude storyboards, inventing imitations of what he had seen.

 Casino suggests that Ace loses power for two reasons: his inability to control Nicky, and his disastrous marriage to Ginger (Sharon Stone). He's attracted to Ginger because of her wildness, first noticing her on the TV monitor as she cheats a client at the tables and then causes a ruckus by throwing his chips in the air. Like Nicky, she seems a good antidote to his overcontrolled nature. She's a cocaine junkie, however, and neurotically tied to an old boyfriend who's now a small-time hustler and pimp, Lester (James Woods). As in *Goodfellas*, there are lots of shots of cocaine sniffing, including an unusual close-up from within a white tube of a line of coke swirling into the tube. Ginger warns Ace about who she is, but his desire for a home life is too strong and he lures her with a fancy house, lots of jewels, and even puts her in sole charge of two million dollars in cash which he keeps as potential pay-off money. The two million seems as much a test of his own commitment as it is of Ginger's. He's reckless about Ginger in a way we see nowhere else. There's an astonishing soft-focus shot of Ace as he stands over Ginger, leaning his head on hers. It's pure corn and suggests a crazy lapse on Scorsese's part until we realize that this is the way Ace wants to see the relationship. The trite use of a pop song when he first sees her is a further indication of his infatuation. Ace, it seems, is naïve around one woman, though tough in all other respects, and though we see him with several other women. Perhaps this is the moral part of him that wants a conventional home life no matter what he does outside the home. Nicky is like this, too; the kindest thing Ace says about him is that he always shows up in the morning to fix his little son breakfast and send him off to school.

Like *Goodfellas*, there's almost wall-to-wall pop music. In part this is appropriate to the super-charged atmosphere of Las Vegas, particularly in the early documentary part of the film when we hear Louie Prima, an actual lounge act, blasting away or Frank Sinatra who was backed by the mob. The music also serves to move the images accompanying Ace's and Nicky's crowded narration along. At many other times the music underlines the obvious. Thus we have Ace's first glimpse of Ginger throwing the chips in the air accompanied by "Baby, My Sweet Baby; You're the One" or "Two to Tango" when Nicky decides to come to Las Vegas and "assist" Ace. "What a Difference a Day Makes" accompanies Ace's presentation to Ginger of a new house stocked with expensive clothes and jewelry. "That's the Glory of Love" is used when Ginger extracts $25,000 from Ace for Lester. There are relatively few sequences without music, such as Nicky's verbal assault on Ace in the desert or Ace's witness to Ginger's phone call to Lester right after their wedding. These seem the more powerful for their spareness. The constant presence of pop music does reflect the fact that the characters are soaked in popular culture and even think in its terms (the soft focus shot of Ace and Ginger). Nicky, the movie buff like Tommy in *Goodfellas*, even makes reference to John Barrymore when referring to Ace's histrionics on his TV show. Still, the moderate musical excesses of *Goodfellas* are grossly exceeded in *Casino*. It's as if Scorsese felt each dramatic incident needed an appropriate accompaniment, as in an opera. Perhaps Robbie Robertson of *Last Waltz* fame had something to do with this; he's listed as music consultant in the credits.

Scorsese's decision to chart the ups and downs of Ace's marriage in exhaustive detail is a mistake. It's clear from the beginning that Ace will have trouble letting Ginger go. The series of arguments they have, though they increase in savagery, are too many and too long. The coarseness and brutality of their exchanges lose punch. The early sequence in which Ginger asks Ace for $25,000 and then won't tell him what it's for goes on for nearly three-and-a-half minutes. It has the spontaneity of an improvised exchange, but it runs on and, like the improvised exchanges between De Niro and Liza Minnelli in *New York, New York* (a far more interesting film), must have been impossible to reduce by cutting. The later scenes of conflict between Ace and Ginger are relieved by some of the comedy that made *Goodfellas* successful, particularly when Ginger gets hold of the safe deposit key and goes after the two million after bashing Ace's car with her Mercedes. The best cinematic treatment of Ginger is the final shot of her death. It's a trademark corridor shot in a grungy hotel as she comes out the door and feels her way along the wall. We're a world away here from the brightly lit, cheerfully garish atmosphere of Las Vegas, and yet it could be argued that this is the world that underlies Las Vegas and that we don't see enough of it.

As Nicky, Joe Pesci repeats the wild dangerousness of his performance as Tommy in *Goodfellas*. He's Ace's opposite; he complements Ace's skills ("I made book and Nicky always collected"), but he also undermines Ace. He runs out the crews who want to rip off the Tangiers, but he subverts the casino by running a loan shark racket with the employees. He can't help himself; his aggressive drives are in total control. He sees himself as a new Al Capone and even takes pride in being banned from the casinos as Capone was. His scenes of conflict with Ace are many—like Ace's scenes with Ginger which they parallel—but they're faster, sharper, more loaded with danger. A good example is the scene in the desert when Nicky threatens Ace for having complained to the bosses about him. Ace is aware that Nicky might kill him, yet he goes out alone and manages to keep his head in response to Nicky's eruption. Pesci gives Nicky a barely controlled rage here. The scene is improvised but it moves briskly and powerfully. Other examples of Nicky's anger are more lurid and drawn out: his attack with a pen on a man in a bar (which is a repeat of the killing of Billy Batts in *Goodfellas*, even down to the squirting blood), his torture of the Irishman whose head he puts in a vice, his threats to a banker who has loaned him money. We're close to the inflated excesses of *Cape Fear* here. His eventual affair with Ginger suggests that he envies Ace and wants what he has—even that he wishes he could become Ace and get beyond his compulsions. This idea is most clearly revealed when Ace goes to a nightclub with his top staff and Nicky eyes him enviously from another table. Nicky's sidekick and "gofer" Frank (unlike Ace, he would have to have a "gofer") remarks that Ace and his crowd are having a good time and Nicky responds with bleak insistence, "Well, so are we." The shot of Nicky and Frank is a direct quote from *Raging Bull* when De Niro and Pesci eye Frank and the bosses from another table. The actor Frank Vincent plays essentially the same role in both films. There's a feeling of repetition here, as well as in the whole treatment of mob culture.

The depiction of Nicky's death is as violent and blood-soaked as his life. In a way, it's the death he's been seeking. The sequence doesn't seem as protracted and garish as, say, the Irishman's torture; it's relatively fast and straight. Frank attacks Nicky from the rear with a baseball bat, and Nicky is then forced to witness the bludgeoning of his brother before he, too, is battered to near death and then thrown (still alive) into a hole in a cornfield. The loyal sidekick, Frank, who was sent out to keep an eye on Nicky just as Nicky was sent out to keep an eye on Ace, has received orders from the bosses. There's no disgruntled poolside retirement in Florida à la Capone for Nicky.

De Niro's performance as Ace is a model of restraint. His careful hand gestures, in particular—finger tips lightly touching—suggest caution and control. His face is usually a composed mask behind which alert eyes move around. Ginger can provoke him to abandon his rational, book-makers' cool, and yet he doesn't seem to have much passion. He is compulsively interested in gambling, but he's not a compulsive gambler. We never see him place a bet. The casino itself is his stake. Nicky's comment that in the old days Ace was so serious about gambling that "he never enjoyed himself" is largely true for his behavior in Las Vegas. He's a taskmaster, firing a slim dancer for being overweight and firing an incompetent slot machine manager for not noticing a tampering incident. This last action is a big mistake because the manager has a relative on the gaming control board and he prevents Ace from obtaining a gambling license. Ace's normal astuteness deserts him here; he could easily transfer the manager to a meaningless job, but he's standing on principle. He won't have his casino run improperly. His tightness, his accountant's soul, damages him. His decision to host a televised talk show from which to attack the gaming control board is a bizarre sign that he's losing his cool. His rage at Ginger is probably at the root of his changed behavior. He seems to move toward Nicky, while Nicky becomes Ginger's cool-headed advisor. The TV show is incredibly dull and it gets the bosses in Kansas City angry. The car bomb attack, which opens and closes the film, is their eventual response. Ace survives as a bookmaker in San Diego.

Ace views Las Vegas as a "morality car wash," in Pileggi's apt phrase. He can do things there and receive community awards that would land him in jail anywhere else. He's not there for self-improvement—or even self-enrichment. He likes the odds. That's why the religious music which frames the film (and the visual fires of damnation in which Ace's body falls) seem out of place. Ace, like the other characters, experiences no spiritual crises, no regeneration. Las Vegas under the mob may be a kind of hell, though glossy, sleek, and full of "amenities," but its powers of purgation produce no inner change. None of the characters has inner conflicts which produce development and growth, like Charlie in *Mean Streets* or Jake in *Raging Bull* or even Henry Hill. Ace, Nicky, Ginger go down in a welter of blood drugs and money. It's a garish spectacle without much internal dimension.

Notes

1. Friedman, *The Cinema of Martin Scorsese*, 175.
2. Keyser, *Martin Scorsese*, 3-6.

Chapter 16

THE BUDDHIST SOUL

KUNDUN, 1998

Kundun is a film of dissolves, creating a flow of images suggesting continuity within change. At first appraisal the film seems an unusual effort for Scorsese. A factually based drama of the current Dalai Lama's early life and escape from Chinese-controlled Tibet, it's the only Scorsese film which deals with a contemporary subject set outside the United States. Moreover, it's a treatment of eastern religion by a deeply western-oriented (not to say Catholic) director. Scorsese's presentation of Tibetan Buddhism is fully convincing. His success was aided in large part by an interesting script by Melissa Mathison who also coproduced the film. Like *The Age of Innocence, Kundun* demonstrates Scorsese's wide range. It's a welcome and liberating change from the mob.

The script depicts the many events in the Dalai Lama's life, from his discovery in 1937 to his departure in 1950. It's divided into four segments: 1937, the discovery of the infant Dalai Lama; 1939, the education of the little boy Dalai Lama; 1944, his life as an older boy; 1949, the Dalai Lama as a young man and his resistance to Mao and departure for India. Because so much ground is covered, the film becomes a succession of quick episodes, of processions, ceremonies, of departures and arrivals, all flowing into one another. There are few extended dramatic scenes and little interior psychological development. It's an eastern film both in content and structure. That said, the film dramatizes the Dalai Lama's spiritual growth with great success and it's here that the film bears Scorsese's signature. The Dalai Lama's struggle from despair in the face of the Chinese takeover to spiritual rebirth is linked to other dramas by Scorsese of the soul's journey through pain and suffering. Jake LaMotta of *Raging Bull* and the Dalai Lama may seem a most unlikely pairing but each is traveling his own pilgrim's progress. *Kundun* has almost no violent passages, however. The Dalai Lama's spiritual growth isn't accompanied by the giving and receiving of physical punishment like LaMotta's. *Kundun* is the only Scorsese film that could be described as "sweet." In its evocation of pacificism the film possesses the quietism of the monk's deep, calm voices, the soft whispering sound of the butter lamps, even the deep vibrating sound of the temple horns. The music by Philip Glass, which might be found repetitive in other settings, is perfect for the Dalai Lama's story. Glass has incorporated the monotone of the horns, the monk's chanting, the sound of the handbells into a score which evokes the contemplative spirit. Scorsese's success in *Kundun* occurs because he makes the strangeness of Tibetan culture seem accessible, intimate—like our own story.

One way intimacy is achieved is by holding down the folkloric element. Tibet is a culture of colorful rituals, music, and costumes, at least to western eyes. Scorsese uses these rituals sparingly. He doesn't want to accentuate the colorful and bizarre. A good example is the appearances of the Nechung oracle. The oracle is a protective deity of Tibet. A tranced monk in full regalia is the medium. The two main appearances of the oracle aren't decorative; they're absolutely necessary to our understanding of the way the Dalai Lama makes decisions. They're also powerful and mesmerizing. The oracle is heavily costumed, with a gigantic headdress. He staggers and spins, supported by a crowd of monks milling around the Dalai Lama's throne. He hisses and spits as he attempts to transmit his message. He is in a heightened state of possession but also close to collapse. The camera pursues him as he weaves through the crowd. In his first appearance he warns of a coming war (with China) and in the second he tells the Dalai Lama to leave Tibet before it's too late, even drawing a crude map of escape. These sequences are wild and chaotic. They make clear the powerful forces working behind the calm, meditative layers of Buddhist life.

Another ritual is even more engrossing: the disposal of the body of the Dalai Lama's father. We see the wrapped body brought to a place in the high mountains where it is dismembered and chunks thrown to the waiting vultures. Scorsese is to be applauded for not pulling his punches here. We see all of the details of dismemberment close up and we see the vultures thrashing at the pieces of meat on the ground and then soaring off into the sky. This common ritual in Tibet emphasizes the natural cycle of death and rebirth. Scorsese's careful, and even devout, handling celebrates the Tibetan way and makes it accessible to us.

In the same way, Scorsese captures perfectly the atmosphere in the Dalai Lama's monastery. These scenes may have been shot in the actual Dungkhar Monastery where the Dalai Lama rested on his way to exile in India. In any case, they are redolent with calm. We see the giant gold statue of a smiling Buddha, eyes lowered, seemingly looking down into the golden haze of the many butter lamps and the monks who sit cross-legged in their meditation. The faint sound of the lamps permeates the air. This setting is evoked at several key moments in the Dalai Lama's life: when he first arrives at the monastery as a child and sees a rat lapping water near the lamps, when he loses his father as a boy, and when as a young man he readies himself for his flight from Tibet. The calm, light-filled effulgence of the space, seen by us at recurring moments, suggests a continuity as well as a deepening of spiritual strength.

Two of the longer dramatic sequences deserve close attention. In the first the infant Dalai Lama is examined and instructed by the sweet monk who discovered him. This is done in the presence of Reting, the regent of Tibet, who had sent out monks to try to find the new spiritual leader. The sequence consists of twenty-one shots and is of particular interest in visual terms. As the monk asks the child, "Can you be a healer for all the sick in the world . . . can you remember?" The child turns and sits at his feet and pulls the monk's rust-colored robe over his head. In shot 5 we see the monk's face dimly through the robe as he instructs, "May I be the protector for those without one?" This shot is reversed in 6 where we see the child's face through the robe. The blurred images, screened by the robe, suggest that these early instructions are not exactly clear to the child. When Reting enters to continue the instruction in shot 10 the child pulls the robe tight across his face, revealing depressions where his mouth and eyes are. In 11 we see Reting, again through the robe, but his image is noticeably clearer. He tells the child the story of the first Dalai Lama, and then addresses the child as *Kundun*, the primal spiritual presence. This moment is accompanied in 17 and 18 by helicopter shots of a river flowing out of the high mountain rock and by the sound of Tibetan horns. Shot 19 gives us a purely abstract shot of blue grains of sand which begin to fluctuate in response to a wind-like force, and 21 shows blue water rippling calmly as the camera moves toward it. We hear Reting's words at this point: "You have chosen to come back to this life once more." The power of this sequence is achieved by the poetic way in which the images reinforce the verbal instruction. The viewer feels that he's sharing in an authentic revelation. The sense of discovery works both ways: the monks are discovering the true Dalai Lama and the child is discovering his spiritual calling. Many of the shots in this sequence are connected by dissolves. Indeed, the dissolve is Scorsese's major cinematic strategy in *Kundun*. No other film in memory has so many. The dissolve functions to give a sense of flow and continuity to a film which covers a large span of time and huge number of events. Dissolves suggest in their interpenetration that everything is connected, as they are in Buddhist philosophy. They also replicate the internal process of continuous change that the Dalai Lama is going through. At one of the Dalai Lama's public appearances Scorsese even uses six fast dissolves to depict his act of sitting on the throne. Glass' score, emphasizing the open-ended structure of "endless songs," complements the dissolves and is appropriate to a film which lacks the usual number of set scenes.

One of Scorsese's more puzzling uses of the camera can be understood in this light. I'm referring to three short sequences in which the camera spins abruptly around corners of buildings. The first occurs as the monks leave the simple mud-walled house where the future Dalai Lama lives with his family. The second occurs at the Dalai Lama's garden residence outside Lhasa, and the third and most important as he leaves at night on his flight to India. These shots show Scorsese at his most expressionistic (as in the fight scenes in *Raging Bull*) but they aren't merely flamboyant gestures as the six dissolves of the Dalai Lama on the throne come close to being. In the third instance the frantic movement of the camera along the wall and around the corner is a fine visual approximation of the anxiety the Dalai Lama is feeling despite his outward calmness. He can't see what lies ahead. Like many of Scorsese's most expressionistic images, they're inside shots.

The other dramatic exchange is more conventional. Now a young man, the Dalai Lama confronts Chairman Mao face to face, against the counsel of his closest advisors who have suggested he flee Tibet. As played by Robert Lin, Mao has a deadly potency. He points out the similarities of Buddhism and communism (lack of class hierarchy, for one) and momentarily convinces the Dalai Lama in their first meeting that they have much in common. But in the second encounter he lectures the young man with saccharine insidiousness, moving his delicate hands in a dance-like rhythm as he shapes his phrases. He's dressed in a frayed uniform but his new black shoes are freshly shined and glistening. He informs the Dalai Lama that Tibet needs to undertake reforms and that "religion is poison." The Dalai Lama receives this oratory with his head down but it's clear that this is a moment of political awakening for him. He'll no longer trust Mao to help Tibet. He's been experiencing his true despair in the wilderness in this visit to China, with nightmares about his lost childhood and his parents' death, and now he must summon himself to resist.

Indeed, the Dalai Lama's developing political awareness is one of the chief—and best dramatized—measures of his growth. The personal and psychological element isn't handled as well in the film. A brief dream sequence is a good example. As the older Dalai Lama sleeps in a temple two Chinese officials speak to him of the sufferings of the Chinese before Mao. These appearances are wooden and occur entirely on a rational plane, though they do demonstrate the Dalai Lama's sympathy for any suffering person. His rapid awareness of Mao's danger can be traced to his earlier political experience in regard to Reting.

It's possible to miss the implications of Reting because the film moves so fast from incident to incident. As the regent, Reting has been governing Tibet in the absence of a new Dalai Lama. When we first see him he's ornately garbed in a gold costume and he takes a pinch of snuff from a delicately crafted container. He's sophisticated and, we learn later, corrupt even though he's a monk. He causes consternation among the Dalai Lama's inner circle because he's asking for so much money and land as a finder's fee for discovering the new Dalai Lama. He evidently lives in a lavish style with lots of women, though we don't see this nor do we see his attempt to overthrow the regent who, earlier as prime minister, had pressed him to go into temporary exile at the behest of the Nechung oracle. All this occurs when the Dalai Lama is a child. He can't be expected to understand Reting's threat without persuasion from his advisors. He likes Reting and believes in his goodness. When he's informed that Reting has been thrown in jail, he's amazed there's a jail in the Potala and then says he wants to visit Reting right away. His advisor's negative reaction, expressed mainly in body language, checks him. He won't override them. The very next sequence confronts him with Reting's death, evidently a speedy suicide, since we see him lying peacefully on the ground in his gold costume.

The political implications of Reting's fall should be clear to the viewer, if they're not entirely so to the Dalai Lama. The advisors and the oracle conspire to bring down a bad man and they do it by circumventing the Dalai Lama because he's only a child. Of course they have nothing but his best interests at heart. They're disinterested monks; Reting is an exception. Nevertheless, there's an implication that the Dalai Lama needs to acquire political consciousness quickly and we watch him do so in his confrontation with the Chinese and particularly with Mao. His advisors may tell him, "Remember you're a monk; don't get mixed up in politics," but he has to learn to function in a political world.

At first the Dalai Lama is committed to pacificism, one of the cardinal tenets of Tibetan Buddhism. He believes that, like Buddha, he can conquer all the devils through enlightenment. As the incidents of Chinese brutality increase he begins to consider resistance, assisted by his advisors who counsel that "nonviolence means cooperation when possible, resistance when it is not." When a Chinese general suggests using the Tibetan army against the people, he raises his voice for one of the first times in the film and says he'll not permit it. Scorsese has him watching the battle scenes from Olivier's *Henry V*, a brilliant adaptation of Shakespeare's play, full of stirring martial speeches and action. He also announces intentions for political reform and tells us: "The saddest thing is: we were about to change . . . we were just about to do it alone." The precise plans for reform are not mentioned, aside from freeing the prisoners, but we are given to understand that they are not the result of pressure from Mao. One can see his backbone stiffening in such incidents.

The Dalai Lama's spiritual growth goes hand in hand with the political. As he matures he grows in inner strength, more and more able to take on the burdens occasioned by the loss of his father and the suffering of his people. He's both distant from them and close to them. We often see him on ceremonial occasions, bending toward them, touching their faces, and we also see him observing them through a telescope from a high window in the Potala. He's very attached to the telescope, taking it with him on his harsh journey. Typical of many Scorsese heroes, suffering makes him stronger. His suffering is not self-inflicted like the others' however. There's even a suggestion that the Dalai Lama has a Christian dimension. This occurs during his flight in a simple shot in which we see the Dalai Lama waking up in a stable and seeing a calf standing over a covered body lying on the stable floor. This reference to Christ's birth seems entirely appropriate to the rebirth the Dalai Lama is experiencing and to the sacrifice he makes for his people.

One of Scorsese's chief strategies for getting inside the Dalai Lama's spirituality is through the use of the sand mandala. There's only one reference to a sand mandala in Mathison's script but Scorsese's visual imagination seized upon it. In its orderliness and symmetry the mandala, in part, is an image of the composed and meditative soul. Of the six references to sand painting in the film, five occur at the end. The first, at the very beginning, is properly speaking, not a mandala; it's a sand painting of Chomolungma (Everest) and we see an image of the great mountain as it dissolves or is wind-swept away into a brightly colored sand replication. This process of disturbance or destruction is what happens in the later sand images, all of which occur during the Dalai Lama's harrowing journey. The first of these later images is calm and orderly but as the journey progresses the other mandalas, particularly five and six, are being destroyed by a hand holding a brush. In Mathison's script the hand belongs to the Dalai Lama. Scorsese omits this and allows the disturbed mandalas to function as images of the Dalai Lama's suffering soul. When we see the Dalai Lama emptying the sand from the destroyed mandala into a lake we're asked to see that he is undergoing a spiritual transformation. His words suggest a sacrifice to relieve the suffering of others: "Thus by the virtue of all that I have done may the pain of every living creature be cleared away."

Scorsese dedicated *Kundun* to the memory of his mother, Catherine, who died the year before the film was released. It evokes with tenderness the spirit of one of the world's great religious leaders. In its chronicle of the early life, it explains the sweet, tough, funny Dalai Lama we have come to know in real life.

Chapter 17

THE URBAN SAINT

BRINGING OUT THE DEAD, 2000

Bringing Out the Dead is Scorsese's most religious film, with the obvious exceptions of *The Last Temptation of Christ* and *Kundun*. This isn't readily apparent from the cinematic text, which describes the harrowing experiences of a paramedic in the urban jungle. The film is based on the novel of the same name by Joe Connelly with a script by Paul Schrader, Scorsese's long-time collaborator, most notably in *Taxi Driver* and *Raging Bull*. The central character, Frank Pierce (Nicolas Cage), is a burned-out saver of lost souls—a secular priest who believes that he's lost the ability to save lives. He's become raw in his constant exposure to suffering, as if his skin has been peeled off and the nerves exposed. His lack of insulation is illustrated in the three-part structure of the film. Each of his paramedic colleagues is protected in one way or another. Larry (John Goodman) in the Thursday section is cushioned by his obsessional appetite for food and by his huge bulk. Still, he's the sanest of the three. Friday's Marcus (Ving Rhames) is enclosed in his born-again Christianity, though he likes to cruise the streets in the ambulance looking at prostitutes. Saturday's Tom (Tom Sizemore) is the craziest of the lot, shielded from pain by his anger and love of bloodshed. He's like Travis Bickle in *Taxi Driver* in his hatred for the low-lifes and scum he deals with. He sees himself as an avenger though he doesn't invoke God's sanction. Frank is the opposite of Bickle and Tom; the suffering and corruption he witnesses provoke his compassion and need to save lives. He's a savior junkie ("Saving someone's life is like falling in love, the best drug in the world. For days afterwards you walk the streets making infinite whatever you see"). In one sense, he's an ideal paramedic, but in another he's not: his lack of insulation makes him unstable, prone to visionary distortion which is well captured in the visuals. His beat is the old neighborhood he grew up in and as he moves through it he says, "It was impossible to pass a building that didn't hold a ghost of something." His sickness of soul is caused in part by his inability to forget. Each companion Larry, Marcus, and Tom is more disturbed than the one before and acts as a measure of (and cause of) Frank's increasing disturbance. Tom's craziness, for instance, influences Frank to bash in car windows, but at the same time we see him moving toward recovery when he revives the suicidal Noel by giving him mouth to mouth resuscitation. He has to go nearly all the way down to come back.

Frank's revival is the main subject of the last part of the film. There are several agents which assist in the process. The first is Mary Burke (Patricia Arquette) the young woman whose father lies near death in the hospital aptly named Our Lady of Infinite Mercy. Mary is no virgin; she is a former drug addict and possibly a former prostitute. Frank's attraction to her helps to get him out of his obsessional introversion but her most crucial agency in his cure lies in his ability to heal her. He rescues her from a drug relapse and gradually elicits a tender response. He saves himself by saving her. The operative literary text here as in other Schrader scripts (like *Taxi Driver*) is Dostoyevsky's *Crime and Punishment.* Like Sonia, Mary is a sinner, but Frank's love for her, like Raskolnikov's, helps him begin the process of purging his guilt. Another agent is Rose, the young woman who haunts Frank more than any of the other ghosts. Frank fails to revive her as she lies in the snow and her loss pierces him like no other. The guilt he feels over Rose and all the others is beginning to be diminished through Mary at the end of the film. Two other agents may be mentioned. The first is Noel (Marc Anthony), the suicidal, dread-lock-wearing man who is a perpetual visitor to the ER. He's viewed as a nuisance by everyone but Frank. When Frank gives him mouth-to-mouth after a savage beating by Tom there's a fairy-tale quality to the incident, like the prince who kisses the old hag and discovers the princess. Frank keeps Noel alive at least until the next inadequate suicide attempt. He can feel his luck beginning to change. Finally, Frank's revival of Cy, the smooth-talking drug dealer who supplies Mary, suggests a definite turning point. It's ironic that the rescue of Cy from his position impaled on a metal fence should be the clearest indicator of improvement. Frank isn't exactly defeating the foe here. Cy is a dangerous man, no matter that he sees himself as a godlike guru dispensing chemical grace at his "oasis." In this respect, *Bringing Out the Dead* is Scorsese's fullest examination of drug use, an element in many of his films, particularly *Goodfellas* and *Casino*. There are two kinds of addiction: Frank's need to save people and Mary's need for hard drugs. Each is a form of excess which can lead to collapse. Frank can't stop working, though he's in a constant state of exhaustion. In one of the few extended verbal passages in the film he explains that after saving someone

> for days, sometimes weeks, afterwards you walk the streets making infinite whatever you see. Once, for a few weeks, I couldn't feel the earth. Everything I touched became lighter. Horns played in my shoes; flowers fell from my pockets. You wonder if you've become immortal, as if you've saved your own life as well. God has passed through you and for a moment there (why deny it) God *was* you.

The playful surrealist touches of the horns and flowers are canceled out by the ghosts he sees of the many he's been unable to save. His spiritual craving is driven by desire to be released from guilt rather than desire for immortality or godlikeness. The dangers of spiritual addiction are almost as severe as drug addiction. In this sense Frank and Mary are both recovering addicts who help each other.

Mary's relapse into drug use is particularly vivid. The setting of Cy's apartment, the "oasis," has been carefully designed, with its deep couches, shag carpeting, red walls, and large aquarium. At one point we see a fish move into contact with a (devouring?) anemone. The fish's languorous movement is a fine visual approximation of the effect of the drug Cy dispenses to Frank who has come to rescue Mary. There's a fine slow pan shot of the room with Cy standing posed by the aquarium, its rhythm expressing Frank's blissed-out state before he goes under. His drug-induced freak-out at Cy's is full of speeded-up shots of street life and the ambulance careening along as well as a replay of the failed attempt to revive Rose in the snow. Rather than calm him, as Cy suggests, the drug brings up all his anxieties. The film's visual distortion is at its high point here, along with the mad behavior of Frank and Tom in the last section.

As I've suggested, Frank's spiritual revival is accompanied by other revivals, not only those of Mary, Noel, and Cy. Mary's father is in a constant state of revival, receiving seventeen episodes of electric shock to the heart to keep him going. We see Frank and Larry administer the shock to him at the opening and see Frank finally release him by disconnecting his breathing tube at the end of the film. Then there's the revival meeting Marcus stages when he and Frank revive an overdosed young man at a drug party where everyone is wearing black clothing and black make-up. Marcus' speech style is full of preacher-like inflections as he dispenses his gospel. Like Cy, Marcus believes that he is extending God's mission. He's like the fundamentalist Christians who tried to disrupt the showings of *The Last Temptation of Christ*. Frank, who isn't sure at all that he's doing God's work successfully, is far stronger.

This summary of the main ideas in the film suggests that it's a dark, heavy experience. It is all that, but it has comic dimensions as well. The best example is Marcus' revival meeting. All the black-clad youngsters are frightened that their young friend is dead from an overdose of cocaine but Frank and Marcus suspect he can be revived by a simple injection. Marcus has the group stand around the body holding hands, their black-rimmed eyes raised toward the ceiling. A close-up of the boy makes him seem transported—a dark angel. When he promptly sits up after the injection and Marcus begins his preaching, the effect is one of comic relief. Another street person, Mr. Oh is presented in comic terms when he's welcomed back to the ER like an old friend. He's an alcoholic who regularly passes out in the street. His neighbors greet Frank and Larry like friends and the dispatcher played by Scorsese in one of his Wellesean voice-only appearances refers to him as "the duke of dump, the king of stink" because of his overpowering odor. A bit earlier, in somewhat forced humor, Scorsese instructs the paramedics to go to a woman who has a roach stuck in her ear and a man who has set his pants on fire. The wild scenes outside the entrance to the ER, in which a large black policeman attempts to keep order, have a kind of comic chaos but it's a black comedy which boils beneath the nightmarish surface. Frank and Tom's attendance upon another perpetual suicide involves Tom pasting an EKG electrode on the man's forehead to cure him. Tom's essential craziness gives his instructions to the disturbed man a bizarre humor. Perhaps the literary text here is Celine's great *Journey to the End of Night*, a novel whose savage black humor is a landmark, and which we see on Frank's bookshelf in the only visit we pay to the place he sleeps when he's not at work. He's a reader and a thinker unlike his colleagues—another reason he's so exposed.

The agitated, driven rhythm of *Bringing Out the Dead* comes from two sources: the unrelieved demands of a paramedic's job and Frank's internal turmoil. We often see overhead shots of the ambulance speeding down the street or close-ups of the headlights or taillights, a la *Taxi Driver*. These traveling shots are accompanied by rock music, giving us a sense of excitement and urgency. As the pressure increases in the Saturday section Scorsese uses strobe lights and even faster cutting. For some viewers such visual and auditory hammering may be too much but Scorsese is trying to put us in Frank's sensibility and give us a replication of the stimuli which bring him to the edge. We've seen the same approach in the boxing scenes in *Raging Bull* or the painting sequences in *Life Lessons*. The attempt in *Bringing Out the Dead,* even more than in the earlier films, is to approximate the derangement of the senses that Frank is experiencing. Thus we have an avalanche of visual distortion than characterizes certain episodes: the camera rolls over nearly 360 degrees as the ambulance speeds away as we hear voices crying out in despair and pain and the pounding rhythm of the music.

The most common sequence is of Frank looking out the window of the ambulance, his gaze rapt, voracious, then a shot or two of what he sees. It's almost always night, the streets are rainslicked, steam rising from the vents, the sidewalk action of prostitutes and johns, under lurid neon or the light of open shops, full of sex and potential violence. These shots remind one of what Travis sees from his taxi in *Taxi Driver*—except that Frank is Travis' opposite. Rose's ghost appears more frequently in the faces of the prostitutes he sees, and in the Friday section he pulls ghosts up as they attempt to emerge from beneath the cobbled street. We're asked to imagine here that these aren't anonymous presences to Frank; that each ghost is a particular person he has failed to revive. His imagination is crowded with the past as well as with the spectacles he witnesses outside the window. They blend together. As Marcus cruises looking at prostitutes and flashing money in the window, Frank tells us, "After a while I grew to understand that my role is less about saving lives than about bearing witness. I was a grief mop. It was enough that I simply showed up." For Frank, the idea of bearing witness means that his own suffering is a redemptive act of taking on the suffering of others. He doesn't ennoble himself, however, as the grief mop comment indicates. He sees himself as just another worker and not all that effective. If you could ask him if he believes in God he might well say he's unsure and that the question is too ultimate, that he's got too much to do right now. He's like one of Ignazio Silone's political saints, or rather he's Scorsese's version of a secular saint, too entangled in suffering and distress to be able to sit calmly above the world in detached pity. Scorsese's Jesus in *The Last Temptation of Christ* would recognize him as a kindred spirit.

Two sequences need a close look. The first captures the film's moments of painful comedy. It's a seventeen-shot passage in which Frank witnesses yet another resuscitation of Mary's father. Frank is beginning to recover his sense of mission, having been told by Cy that he saved his life. His face is fresher, more alert as he peers over the doctor's shoulder. The second shot is the first of a group of six in the sequence in which we look down on the father from Frank's and the doctor's point of view. He's angry, struggling upward against the breathing tube taped to his mouth. As Frank and the doctor begin to talk about how many he's "coded" (seen as essentially dead) and then brought back by defibrillation, the father's look of agitated resentment increases. When the conversation turns to joking about sending him home with a defibrillator so he can shock himself alive, there's a poignant medium shot of the old man lying back in despair. It's clear that he understands everything though he's near death. He's like Cy, gravely wounded but fully conscious. In this sense, the film portrays dying as a conscious experience of resistence, of clinging to life. As the joking intensifies, the father resumes his angry protest, though in the last two of the six shots this shades into an amazing participation in the humor. There's a fierce gaiety in his eyes and the soundtrack intensifies the laughter by adding wild laughing (which sounds like Scorsese's) to that of Frank and the doctor. The sequence concludes with a rapper's voice informing us that "it ain't funny." But it is.

The second sequence is the last in the film and involves Frank's visit to Mary to inform her that her dad is dead. As he stands talking to Mary in her doorway he sees Rose's wan face. She tells him that "we have to keep the body going until the brain and arm recover enough to go on their own." This bizarre, dreamlike comment probably has something to do with Frank's guilt at having released the father as well as his guilt about her. It's also a repeat of Frank's words to Mary about her father early in the film. Rose is comforting him, not accusing him. When he says, "Forgive me, Rose," Mary, whom we see in the next shot, doesn't acknowledge that he isn't talking to her. This seems an oversight until we realize she's deep in her own grieving. After he tells her he saved Noel she invites him in and in the last shot we see Frank leaning against her as she sits. It seems a freeze-frame until we see Mary slowly move her hand from his shoulder to his head. The shot slowly begins to whiten until a full brilliant light fills the screen. This glowing ending has been prepared by a series of shots in which a character (usually Rose) takes on a bright nimbus and by Frank's comment that "when good happens everything glows."

This calm touching ending to such a harsh film doesn't say that Frank is healthy, only that with Mary's help he can begin revival. He has the chance gradually to let go of his ghost-ridden life, to begin to see Mary, not Maryrose.

As in many of Scorsese's films, Frank's story ends at the very beginning of his spiritual revival. He's like Jake LaMotta in the nightclub dressing room at the very end or even like Travis Bickle when Betsy gets in his cab—with the obvious exception that he hasn't dispensed violence upon others. He's never been a great sinner as a prelude to enlightenment. The violence he's done to himself exists in his addiction to suffering. He's more like the Dalai Lama in the desire to take on the suffering of others—but without the Buddhist calmness and loss of ego. He's our Western saint.

Conclusion

Scorsese's best work examines our urban violence and angst. The nearly total absence of nature, of landscape, as both a destructive and consoling presence—a major element in American life and film—is an indication of his absorption in the urban environment. His imagined city, whether the genteel New York of *The Age of Innocence* or the contemporary city of small-time hoods in *Mean Streets*, is full of treachery and potential disaster. The city exalts as much as it defeats. As Cy, the drug dealer in *Bringing Out the Dead*, exclaims as he lies high above the street, impaled on an iron railing, "I love this city!" The counter voice is Mary's in the same film: the city is brutal, you can only survive if you're tough. The city, with its rain-slicked streets, steam coming up from the grates, its grimy hallways, is Scorsese's crucible—the visual space in which his characters act out their drama of spiritual regeneration through violence and suffering. That he should choose it is no accident given his immigrant parents' struggle to survive within it. His childhood seems to have determined many of his later choices: his fascination with tough guys like Jake LaMotta in *Raging Bull*, or violent undergroundlings like Travis Bickle in *Taxi Driver* or Rupert Pupkin in *King of Comedy*, or his many forays into mob behavior as in *Goodfellas* and *Casino*. The 2002 *Gangs of New York* is further indication of this pattern. His central characters, as I've pointed out, are almost always driven, compulsive males like Lionel Dobie in *Life Lessons* and much of his brilliant, expressionistic camera work is an attempt to evoke their inner states. This expressionism is balanced by an equally strong documentary impulse. The viewer knows the factual environment of his characters' lives as well as their, often tormented, souls. It's a complete and engrossing presentation. When he chooses to move away from his usual subject matter as in *The Age of Inno-*

cence and *Kundun*, Scorsese does fine work and demonstrates the range of his sensibility. This is particularly true of *Kundun*, with its calm, sweet, meditative style.

Nothing has been said in this brief study about Scorsese's work to promote excellence in film culture. He's the dean of American film, promoting young filmmakers by lending his name and sometimes his money, making documentaries about film of all kinds (Italian film, early American film, film noir), granting endless interviews in which he brings to bear his encyclopedic knowledge—and nearly photographic memory—of film. He's not only one of our best filmmakers; he's the best teacher of film we've ever had. He's done for film what Leonard Bernstein did for music in his various televised lectures a few years ago. A good book could be written about this aspect alone of Scorsese's work.

If his work is too violent for some tastes it has to be said that, with the exception of *Cape Fear* and *Gangs of New York*, his presentation of violence is honest and straight rather than the entertaining violence of most of American film. Our popular culture is saturated by sex and violence as a form of fun. In *Mean Streets*, *Taxi Driver*, *Raging Bull*, *The King of Comedy*, and *Goodfellas*, among others, Scorsese says violence is horrifying, psychologically scarring—as it really is. One doesn't leave his films saying merely, "I had a good time," as a prelude to forgetting the experience. His best films stay with us, inhabit our imaginations.

Has an obsession with violent toughs been good for Scorsese's art? If one thinks of *Cape Fear* and even of *Casino* and *Gangs of New York*, the answer is no. *Raging Bull* and *Goodfellas*, however, are triumphant answers in the affirmative. The obsession is both a limitation and a source of vital emotional and artistic energy. In this sense Scorsese is like many fine writers who have written the same novel again and again in a series of brilliant variations (Dostoyevsky, Conrad, James, Joyce, Faulkner, Marquez. . . .). Viewed in this light, his repetition is like reaching down to the source, the taproot, before going on to other projects. The danger, of course, is that Scorsese has typecast himself. That may account for why some critics found *The Age of Innocence* and *Kundun* deficient. They wanted Scorsese to be Scorsese the mob guy, the tough guy. *The Age of Innocence* and *Kundun* aren't as good as *Taxi Driver*, *Raging Bull*, and *Life Lessons*, but they are fine films which reveal that Scorsese has years of continued growth and change ahead of him.

Postscript: *Gangs of New York*

Gangs of New York was released in 2003 as this book was about to go to press. Scorsese had read Herbert Asbury's book of the same title in 1970 and began script work in 1975. The book is a vivid, entertaining, half-fiction chronicle of the criminal gangs that congregated mainly in an area known as Five Points in the 1860s and '70s. Like TV cop dramas and "reality shows" today, it provided a frisson for an audience who felt basically secure in their homes and neighborhoods. Scorsese's inability to let the project go despite many reversals suggests that it had a particularly deep hold on his imagination. His determination to make an enormously expensive movie of the book (over $110 million by most reports) stems at bottom from his childhood infatuation with larger-than-life tough guys like Dirty Face Jack, Socco the Bracer, Kid Shanahan, Pugsy Hurley, and Bill the Butcher. Unfortunately *Gangs of New York* isn't a very good movie. It's long on spectacle and short on involving depth despite its evocation of a particular place and historical moment.

Asbury's book has almost no narrative dimension; it moves quickly from one gang to another and doesn't tell stories. The central characters of the film, Bill the Butcher (Daniel Day-Lewis) and Amsterdam Vallon (Leonardo DiCaprio), are given two pages at the most. Jay Cocks' script concocts the long-running story of Vallon's revenge against Bill for his father's murder. At two hours and forty-seven minutes, it's by far Scorsese's longest film. Vallon witnesses the murder as a child then returns some fifteen years later to deal with Bill but finds himself falling under Bill's charismatic influence. In effect Bill has become a kind of substitute father, neutralizing Vallon's zeal. The father-son relationship is the thematic center of the film. Vallon hasn't really grown up; he's looking for a father and makes the poor choice of Bill—or, more accurately,

165

allows himself to be chosen by Bill. Perhaps this accounts for DiCaprio's rather pallid and passive performance. In contrast Day-Lewis delivers a splendid rendering of a murderous, commanding gang leader. Squinting out of his one good eye, growling and swaggering under his stovepipe hat, he seems right off the Elizabethan stage. It's an exaggerated performance that explains why Vallon falls under his influence. It also explains why he's a man who deserves killing.

Bill's gang, called the natives, stands for the racial purity of indigenous Americans and against the pollution of immigrants. Vallon's father, Priest Vallon, leads the dead rabbits who represent the newly arrived Irish. The battle between these two groups occurs throughout the film and is chiefly represented by two encounters in which the ranks of fighters stand behind the leaders who make rousing speeches before the bloodshed begins. We've seen such scenarios many times before—in Westerns and war films—and the avoidance of cinematic cliché is difficult and Scorsese doesn't escape it. In the battle which opens the film the furious montage of stabbings and clubbings is rendered with gusto. It's choreographed violence with certain killings shot at modified slow motion. The cliché of the leaders somehow finding each other in the midst of such chaos is enacted when Bill kills Priest Vallon and at the end when Vallon kills Bill. The fist fight between Vallon and McGlooin, one of Bill's henchmen, is heavily choreographed and conventional. Scorsese's treatment of violence in *Gangs* is stagey, formulaic, and "entertaining"—much like the violence in *Cape Fear*. It lacks the piercing thrust of the violence in *Taxi Driver* and *Raging Bull*. Did the huge budget persuade him to attempt another crowd-pleaser? If so, the strategy didn't pay off. *Gangs* had a tepid reception at the box office and went quickly to video. Only one violent sequence has the punch of the earlier films: the thirteen fast shots in which Vallon struggles on the floor with a would-be assassin of Bill, fighting him for the gun and then shooting him. This brief episode has the rawness of Travis Bickle's murder of the mob collection man on the floor of Iris' room at the end of *Taxi Driver*. It may have actually been modeled on that sequence.

Other cinematic clichés are overused. On three separate occasions Scorsese has the camera shoot behind doors as they fly open (with accompanying noise in the soundtrack) revealing a scene of pandemonium into which the camera moves. Bill is a genius with a knife. The scene in which he uses a pig's carcass to instruct Vallon on how to stab a man ("This is a wound") has elemental force but Scorsese gets carried away with Bill's prowess. He unbelievably deflects the knife Vallon throws at him by throwing a knife himself. And when he has Vallon spread out for dismemberment on a table he throws a cleaver into the air. Scorsese's camera tracks the cleaver as it spins using slow motion and intercutting with reaction shots of the rapt audience. It's crude theater and it's even cruder when Bill puts on a performance of knife throwing using Vallon's lover Jenny as target, with even more reaction shots. This is straight out of the carney sideshow.

The revival of the dead rabbits under Vallon's leadership is presented in religious terms. We see an assembly of men, women, and children holding candles and Vallon kissing the Celtic cross, but the sequence is so brief as to feel perfunctory and laid on. How did the revenge-minded Vallon manage to rebuild a shattered movement? How does he move away from Bill's influence and become a religious leader like his father? The film is so busy moving from one dramatic incident to another that it doesn't explore this intimate dimension. It remains on the level of spectacle.

Scorsese's attempts at historical accuracy do give *Gangs* some real value. We see the Civil War intermittently as a backdrop to the gangland action—coffins laid out on the docks, an actor playing Abraham Lincoln attacked with fruit thrown by the audience, and, most of all, a vivid depiction of the riots in which common people who couldn't come up with $300 rebelled against being drafted into the army. We also see glimpses of the racial savagery which accompanied the draft riots: African-Americans being stabbed and lynched. Photographs of the Civil War dead by Mathew Brady and his team are used, as are sketches of the riots which appeared in the press. As one would expect from Scorsese, the period details of costume and music are carefully observed. This can be seen in one of the best sequences in which the camera follows a singer as he enters a dance hall to the tune of "New York Girls" and finds Jenny choosing a partner by looking in a mirror as the men approach behind her. Enormous care was given to production details by Dante Ferretti who had earlier demonstrated his skill in the weightier *The Age of Innocence*. Oddly enough for a director whose interest in tribal mores is well known, the sociology of gang behavior in *Gangs* is explored far less than in *Mean Streets*, *Raging Bull*, *Goodfellas*, or *Casino*. The plug uglies, the dead rabbits and their brethren are used mainly for their color. Scorsese's *Gangs* captures the tabloid energy of Asbury's book but doesn't go much beyond it.

Bibliography

Asbury, Herbert. *The Gangs of New York.* New York: Blue Ribbon Books, 1939.

Biskind, Peter. "Slouching Toward Hollywood." *Premier* (December 1991): 60-73.

Bliss, Michael. *Martin Scorsese and Michael Cimino* . Metuchen, N.J.: Scarecrow Press, 1985.

———. *The Word Made Flesh: Catholicism and Conflict in the Films of Martin Scorsese.* Lanham, Md.: Scarecrow Press, 1995.

Bruce, Bryan. "Martin Scorsese: Five Films." *Movie* 31/32 (1986): 88-94.

Cieutat, Michel. *Martin Scorsese.* Paris: Rivages, 1988.

Ciment, Michael. "Les Enfants Terribles." *American Film* 10 (1984): 36-42, 86, 91.

Ciment, Michael, and Michael Henry. "Entretien avec Martin Scorsese." *Positif* 170 (June 1975): 8-23.

Connelly, Marie Katheryn. *Martin Scorsese.* Jefferson, N.C.: McFarland, 1993.

Corliss, Richard. "Body and Blood: An Interview with Martin Scorsese." *Film Comment* (October 1988): 36-42.

Dougan, Andy. *Martin Scorsese* . New York: Thunder's Mouth Press, 1998.

Ebert, Roger. *The Future of Movies: Interviews with Martin Scorsese, Steven Spielberg and George Lucas.* Kansas City, Mo.: Andrews and McMeel, 1991.

Ehrenstein, David. *The Scorsese Picture.* New York: Carol Publishing Group, 1992.

Friedman, Lawrence S. *The Cinema of Martin Scorsese.* New York: Continuum Publishing Co., 1998.

Greeley, Andrew. *The Catholic Imagination*. Berkeley: University of California Press, 2000.

Grist, Leighton. *The Films of Martin Scorsese, 1963-77*. New York: St. Martin's Press, 2000.

Holdenfield, Chris. "Martin Scorsese: The Art of Non-Compromise." *American Film* (March 1989): 46-51.

Jacobs, Diane. *Hollywood Renaissance*. New York: Dell Publishing Co., 1980.

Kazantzakis, Nikos. *The Last Temptation of Christ*. New York: Simon & Schuster, 1960.

Kelly, Mary Pat. *Martin Scorsese, The First Decade*. Pleasantville, N.Y.: Redgrave Publishing Co., 1980.

———. *Martin Scorsese: A Journey*. New York: Thunder's Mouth Press, 1991.

Keyser, Les. *Martin Scorsese*. New York: Twayne Publishing Co., 1992.

Kolker, Robert Philip. *A Cinema of Loneliness*. New York: Oxford University Press, 1988.

LaMotta, Jake. *Raging Bull*. Secaucus, N.J.: Lyle Stuart, 1986.

Lourdeaux, Lee. *Italian and Irish Filmmakers in America*. Philadelphia, Pa.: Temple University Press, 1990.

McGreal, Jill. "Mean Streets." *Sight and Sound* (1993): 3, 64.

Monaco, James. *American Film Now*. New York: Zoetrope, 1984.

Naremore, James. *Acting in the Cinema*. Berkeley: University of California Press, 1988, 262-285.

Pileggi, Nicholas. *Wiseguy*. New York: Simon & Schuster, 1985.

Sangster, Jim. *Scorsese*. London: Virgin Books, 2002.

Schrader, Paul. *Schrader on Schrader*. London: Faber and Faber, 1990.

———. *Taxi Driver*. London: Faber and Faber, 1990.

Scorsese, Martin. "Entretien avec Martin Scorsese: Les rues de New York sont toujours peuplées de fantômes" (Interview with Michael Henry on *Bringing Out the Dead*). *Positif* 18, 470-473.

———. *Kundun* (Interview with Gavin Smith). *Film Comment* (January 1, 1998): 8-22.

———. *Martin Scorsese: Interviews*. Peter Brunette, ed. Jackson, Miss.: University of Mississippi Press, 1999.

———. *A Personal Journey with Martin Scorsese through American Movies*. New York: Miramax Books, 1997.

———. *Scorsese on Scorsese*. London: Faber and Faber, 1989.

Singer, Mark. "The Man Who Forgets Nothing." *New Yorker* (March 27, 2000): 90-103.

Smith, Steven C. *A Heart at Fire's Center: The Life and Music of Bernard Herrmann*. Berkeley: University of California Press, 1991.

Stern, Lesley. *The Scorsese Connection*. Bloomington, Ind.: Indiana University Press, 1995.

Taubin, Amy. *Taxi Driver*. Berkeley: University of California Press, 2000.

Thomson, David. *A Biographical Dictionary of Film*. New York: Knopf, 1994, 677-679.

Tirard, Laurent.*Moviemaker's Master Class*. New York: Faber and Faber, 2002.

Weiss, Marion. *Martin Scorsese: A Guide to References and Resources*. Boston, Mass.: G. K. Hall, 1987.

Wharton, Edith. *The Age of Innocence*. New York: Macmillan Publishing Co., 1992.

Index

Abbott, Diahnne, 55, 58
Acting in the Cinema, 81
After Hours, 85-92, 128
The Age of Innocence, xvi, 12, 13, 22, 131-137, 148, 163, 164, 167
Alice Doesn't Live Here Anymore, 28, 31-35, 98
Allen, Woody, 110
American Boy, 29, 30, 47, 61-63
And God Created Woman, 88
Anthony, Marc, 157
Arquette, Patricia, 156
Arquette, Rosanna, 87, 111
Asbury, Herbert, 165, 167
Au Hazard Balthazar, 102
Austen, Jane, 132

Balsam, Martin, 126
The Band, 58-61
Bardot, Brigitte, 88
"Before the Law," 89
Benny, Jack, 81
Bergman, Ingmar, 10, 106
Bernhard, Sandra, 80, 81
Bernstein, Elmer, 126
Bethune, Zina, 8, 13, 128
The Big Shave, 5-7
A Biographical Dictionary of Film, 123n

Bonnie and Clyde, 15, 16, 48
Bosch, Hieronymous, 71, 107
Boxcar Bertha, 15-19, 34, 107
Boyle, Peter, 40
Bracco, Lorraine, 117, 128
Bresson, Robert, 102
Bringing Out the Dead, 17, 28, 155-161, 163
Brooks, Albert, 40
Burstyn, Ellen, 31, 98
Butterfield, Paul, 58

Cage, Nicolas, 156
Campion, Jane, 131
Cape Fear, 10, 13, 15, 17, 22, 34, 125-130, 131, 141, 143, 164, 166
Capone, Al, 143, 144
Carradine, David, 16, 102
Carradine, John, 16
Casino, 22, 30, 121, 139-145, 157, 163, 164, 167
Cassavetes, John, 16
Celine, Louis-Ferdinand, 71, 159
Champion, 71
Cheech and Chong, 86
Cocks, Jay, 131, 136, 165
The Color of Money, 34, 93-99, 126, 141
Connelly, Joe, 156

Coppola, Francis Ford, 110
Corman, Roger, 15, 16, 21
Crime and Punishment, 44, 49, 157
Cruise, Tom, 94
Cul de Sac, 77

Dafoe, Willem, 104
Dalai Lama, 147-153, 161
Dali, Salvador, 18
Day-Lewis, Daniel, 22, 132, 165, 166
De Kooning, Willem, 112
De Niro, Robert, 22, 37, 41, 43, 44, 52, 65, 66, 67, 68, 69, 77, 78, 79, 81, 83, 116, 121, 126, 127, 130, 140, 143, 144
Diamond, Neil, 59, 61
DiCaprio, Leonardo, 165
Diebenkorn, Richard, 112
Disney Studios, 126, 129
Donne, John, 105
Dostoyevsky, Fyodor, 44, 110, 157
Douglas, Kirk, 71
Dunne, Griffin, 85
Dunphy, Don, 73
Dylan, Bob, 58, 60

Ebb, Fred, 52
The Executioners, 126

Farentino, Linda, 87
Fellini, Frederico, 5, 23
Ferretti, Dante, 132, 167
Forster, E. M., 132
Foster, Jodie, 43, 49, 128
Friedman, Lawrence, 34, 97, 141

Gabriel, Peter, 107
The Gambler, 110
Gangs of New York, 163, 164, 165-167
Garr, Teri, 88
Glass, Philip, 148, 150
Godard, Jean-Luc, 6, 8, 10
The Godfather, 115, 119, 120

Goodfellas, 12, 22, 29, 68, 115-123, 128, 136, 139, 141, 142, 143, 157, 163, 164, 167
Goodman, John, 156
The Gospel According to St. Matthew, 102

Harris, Emmy Lou, 60
Helm, Levon, 58, 59, 60
Henry V, 152
Herrmann, Bernard, 13, 46, 48, 126, 130
Hershey, Barbara, 16, 102, 104, 105
High Noon, 94
Hope, Bob, 81
Hopkins, Anthony, 129
The Horse's Mouth, 112
The Hustler, 93, 94, 95, 98

Italianamerican, 1, 28-30
It's Not Just You, Murray!, 4-5

James, Henry, 131, 132, 136
Journey to the End of Night, 159
Judd, Donald, 112

Kael, Pauline, 21
Kafka, Franz, 89, 90, 91
Kander, John, 52
Kazantzakis, Nicos, 101, 102, 106
Keitel, Harvey, 8, 13, 22, 32, 33, 39, 104, 118, 140
Keyser, Les, 8, 141
King of Comedy, 22, 49, 52, 77-84, 85, 110, 129, 163, 164
Kristofferson, Kris, 33, 41
Kundun, xvi, 13, 147-153, 155, 164

LaMotta, Jake, 65-75, 148
Lange, Jessica, 126
The Last Laugh, 28
The Last Temptation of Christ, 13, 16, 17, 19, 85, 98, 101-108, 155, 158, 160

The Last Waltz, 58-61, 142
Las Vegas, 140, 141, 142
Lewis, Jerry, 77
Lewis, Juliette, 127, 130
Life Lessons, 6, 14, 94, 98, 109-114, 135, 163, 164
Life Without Zoe, 110
Lin, Robert, 151
Liotta, Ray, 22, 116

MacDonald, John, 126
The Magnificent Ambersons, xv
Manoogian, Haig, 2, 8, 74
Marden, Bryce, 112
Martin, Mardik, 4
Mathison, Melissa, 148, 153
Mean Streets, 2, 7, 8, 11, 12, 17, 21-28, 29, 30, 31, 39, 68, 98, 118, 128, 129, 140, 145, 163, 164, 167
Minion, Joseph, 85
Minnelli, Liza, 52, 128, 143
Minnelli, Vincente, 51, 56
Mitchell, Joni, 58, 59
Mitchum, Robert, 126, 127
Moriarty, Cathy, 68, 69, 128
Morrison, Van, 58, 59
Mouchette, 102
Murnau, F. W., 28

Naremore, James, 81
Newman, Paul, 93, 94, 97, 98
New York, New York, 13, 26, 51-57, 58, 59, 74, 110, 128
New York Stories, 109, 110
Nolte, Nick, 110, 126
Notes from the Underground, 44

Oedipus Wrecks, 110
Olivier, Laurence, 152
Ovitz, Michael, 102

Paramount Studios, 102
Pasolini, Piero, 102
Peck, Gregory, 126

Peckinpah, Sam, 48
Persona, 106
Pesci, Joe, 22, 68, 69, 116, 120, 121, 140, 143, 144
Pfeiffer, Michelle, 22, 132
Pileggi, Nicholas, 115, 116, 117, 139, 145
Polanski, Roman, 77, 91
Pollock, Jackson, 112
The Portrait of a Lady, 131
Powell, Michael, 2
Pressburger, Emeric, 2
Price, Richard, 94, 110, 111
Prince, Stephen, 47, 61-62
Puccini, Giacomo, 113
Puzo, Mario, 115

Raging Bull, 3, 6, 12, 14, 22, 28, 30, 61, 65-75, 78, 82, 97, 98, 99, 107, 109, 110, 112, 127, 128, 129, 144, 145, 148, 151, 156, 159, 163, 164, 166, 167
The Red Shoes, 2
Rhames, Ving, 156
Rickles, Don, 81
Rio Bravo, 10
Robertson, Robbie, 58, 60, 61, 142
Robinson, Amy, 128
Robinson, Sugar Ray, 66, 67, 69, 71, 72-73
Rocco and His Brothers, 23, 47
Rossen, Robert, 93, 98
Ryder, Winona, 132, 136

Schoonmaker, Thelma, 59, 73
Schrader, Paul, 37, 38, 41, 42, 50, 65, 66, 67, 102, 104, 156, 157
Scorsese, Catherine, 1, 5, 8, 29, 153
Scorsese, Charles, 1, 29
Scorsese on Scorsese, 1, 18, 75n
Scorsese, Martin,
    absense of nature, 10, 163
    documentary realism, 6, 22-23, 25, 28, 29-30, 43, 48, 62, 69-70, 90-91, 115,

140-141, 163
early life, 1-3
expressionism, 28, 39, 40, 66,
    69, 70-73, 74, 90-91,
    151, 163
machismo, 10, 11, 24, 28, 141
misogyny, 11-12, 27, 28, 91,
    127-128, 136
religious dedication to film, 2,
    74, 110, 114
use of improvization, 13, 22,
    26, 53-54, 62, 70, 143
use of music, 12-13, 118
violence, 129-130, 164, 166
violence and religion, 8-9, 19,
    24, 27, 49, 66, 74, 145,
    163
The Searchers, 9
Shakespeare, William, 152
Shepherd, Cybill, 39, 128
Shick, Wesley, 126
The Silence of the Lambs, 129
Silone, Ignazio, 160
Sizemore, Tom, 156
Smoke, 11
Sorvino, Paul, 120
Spielberg, Steven, 126
Stanton, Harry Dean, 106
Stone, Sharon, 141

Taxi Driver, 6, 13, 14, 17, 22, 28,
    37-50, 51, 61, 62, 83, 91, 104,
    109, 110, 122, 128, 129, 130,
    156, 157, 159, 163, 164, 166
Teamsters Union, 140
The Tenant, 77, 91
The Thief of Baghdad, 2

Thompson, J. Lee, 125, 126
Thomson, David, 123n
Tibetan Buddhism, 148, 152
The Trial, 17, 90, 91
Truffaut, Francois, 10
Turandot, 113

Ufland, Harry, 102
United Artists, 102
Universal Studios, 102, 126

Vadim, Roger, 88
Vale, Jerry, 121
Van Sant, Gus, 117
Vincent, Frank, 144
Visconti, Luchino, 23, 47
Vitelloni, 23

Warner, Frank, 73
Wayne, John, 9, 10
Welles, Orson, xv, 17, 90, 158
Wharton, Edith, 131, 132, 136
*What's a Nice Girl Like You Doing
    in a Place Like This?*, 3-4
Whitaker, Forest, 96
Who's That Knocking at My Door?,
    3, 7-14, 15, 22, 24, 27, 30, 39,
    128
Wiseguy, 115
Woods, James, 141
Woodstock, 15
Woodward, Joanne, 132

Young, Neil, 58, 59

Zimmerman, Paul, 77, 78